Adobe Photoshop 3.03
1 Photo CD / Disk 1 / 5
S/N : PWW30DR30

Mai Cao
368-6584

The Battle to Stay Competitive
Changing the Traditional Workplace

The Delco Moraine NDH Story

The Battle To Stay Competitive
Changing the Traditional Workplace

The Delco Moraine NDH Story

Charles R. Birkholz
and
Jim Villella

Productivity Press
Cambridge, Massachusetts
Norwalk, Connecticut

Originally published as *"If You Ain't the Lead Dog, the Scenery Never Changes"* by Delco Moraine NDH.

All rights reserved. No part of this book may be reproduced or utilized in any form or by any means, electronic or mechanical, including photocopying, recording, or by any information storage and retrieval system, without permission in writing from the publisher. Additional copies are available from the publisher. Address all inquiries to:

Productivity Press
P.O. Box 3007
Cambridge, Massachusetts 02140
United States of America
(617) 497-5146 (telephone)
(617) 868-3524 (telefax)

Cover design by Kathlin Sweeney
Interior design and composition by David Lennon
Printed and bound by Goodway Graphics
Printed in the United States of America

Library of Congress Cataloging-in-Publication Data

Birkholz, Charles R.
 The battle to stay competitive: changing the traditional workplace: the Delco Moraine NDH story/Charles R. Birkholz and Jim Villella.
 ISBN 0-915299-73-9 (pbk.)
 1. Delco Moraine NDH. 2. Automobile supplies industry — United States. 3. Quality circles — United States. 4. Automobiles — Brakes — Quality control. 5. Competition — United States. I. Villella, Jim. II. Title.
 HD9710.3.U54D462 1990
 338.7'629246'0973 — dc20   90-19195
                                                                    CIP

91 92 93 10 9 8 7 6 5 4 3 2 1

*Dedicated to the Memory of Ron Stump
and His Support of Our Efforts*

TABLE OF CONTENTS

Preface ix
Introduction xi
The Vision of Cultural Change
At the Needmore Road Plant by Our Plant Manager xiii

Section I Soft-Side Activities

1   Initial Activities 1
2   Mainstreaming the Participative Process 7
3   Participative vs Permissive 13
4   Grass Roots Observation of Change 19
5   A Taste of Success 33

Section II Hard-Side Activities

6   A Key to Technical Change:
     Three Sides of the Organization 37
7   Continuous Improvement 43
8   Key Elements of the Synchronous Process 49
9   Our Measurement System 75
10 Accomplishments to Date 93

About the Authors 97

PREFACE

This book attempts to define a non-traditional approach to a common problem in business — the threat of competition and potential loss of market share. This problem and related solutions encompass problem recognition, assessment of facts, organization of a game plan, and implementation of that plan to resolve the problem. Inherent in the problem-solving process is the implementation of *change*, both cultural and technological.

The kinds of changes we wish to address are those that go beyond day-to-day changes. Changes that address not only the market pressures of today, but those that recommend a total cultural change for a work force that has thrived on an adversarial relationship for several decades.

The necessity for change was brought about by significant competitive events that have placed U.S. organizations in a survival threatening mode. These events have forced us to choose between short-term decisions (focused only on the immediate future and the bottom line) versus the knowlege that we must invest in our future.

Any change effort that goes beyond the normal reshuffling of the key players involves an enormous amount of energy and monetary resources. These efforts are generally limited in any business enterprise and thus must be expended where the greatest potential return can be anticipated.

Obviously, as the following chapters will confirm, the problems involved in this type of change are in no way unique to General Motors. The American manufacturing arena is facing similar problems and implementing similar solutions.

It is our intent to share some of our change efforts along with the successes and mid-course corrections that had to be made. The various lessons that resulted from our change efforts, as well as the steps that we are currently implementing, will assure Delco Moraine NDH a position in today's marketplace as a *world-class supplier* of automotive components.

INTRODUCTION

Over the past decade Delco Moraine NDH (General Motor's Brake Systems Division) has been slowly and painfully dealing with the harsh reality that they are competing in a marketplace populated with many more competitors who have a strong awareness and sensitivity for quality and value and selling to consumers who are demanding the same. This challenge to compete in the open marketplace is new in the automotive industry and especially with the GM component divisions.

With this challenge as part of our everyday business life, we as a division (like so many others) have developed and tried several processes and experiments to improve our *quality, delivery* and *cost*. Some have been looked upon as failures, some as successes, but in most cases they have all led to positive cultural changes in the pursuit of an identity as a world class supplier. Additionally each effort has given us a broader base of awareness and understanding upon which to build our future efforts.

Much of the automotive story has been told on the six-thirty evening news, in national newspapers and magazines, as well as on specials such as the NBC *"White Papers."* Our attempt here is to chronicle the *"floor level"* or grass roots activities that have given our division a competitive edge and our people a reason to be proud of the contributions they are making.

My personal involvement began in February 1984 when I was appointed to the position of Quality of Work Life Coordinator (Q.W.L.). Prior to this time, I was a General Supervisor in the Disc Brake Manufacturing Operations. As a General Supervisor, I knew little about the Q.W.L. change efforts that had been in progress over the past two years. My Superintendent at some point in time had suggested that I investigate and start Employee Participation Groups (EPGs) in our area. When I asked what they were, he stated, *"I don't know, but you should start some."* I succeeded in ignoring the process and its benefits for two years and was fully convinced that based on the performance numbers we were generating in our operations that there was no need for changes and that our employees were basically satisfied with their performance and the contributions they were making. We were saving money in our burden accounts, generating a respectable savings in our cost reduction programs, maintaining our goals in operating efficiency, and achieving inventory turns of ten to eleven per year. Most of all, we were making a *profit*. Little did we know how narrow our focus was and how soon our competitive position would be eroded.

As I assumed the role of Q.W.L. Coordinator, I quickly realized that my mission took on a broader perspective as a *change agent*. At the UAW Walter and Mae Reuther Black Lake Training Center, I heard leadership from both the International Union and the G.M. Corporate Staff detail the need for changes. Locally, I heard UAW Vice President Don Ephlin and Irv Bluestone (Past Vice President of the UAW and now Professor at Wayne State University) reinforce the same needs. Additional exposure at The International Association of Quality Circle Conferences, GM consultant Conferences and University Associates Workshops, indicated that change was being pursued by both the public and private economic community far beyond what I had anticipated.

These efforts were loaded with uncertainties. What was the focus of this change effort? What was its significance? To whom was it directed? What was the proof of the need that justified the monies and energy committed at the Corporate and the International Union levels? Just how far ranging was it going to be? More importantly, was this just *another program* moving down the aisle and out the back door like so many others in the past.

The answers are in the stories, the illustrations, the lessons, the breakthroughs, and the commitments which we wish to share. They did not come about without a fair amount of grief and effort on the part of many of the employees of Delco Moraine NDH, so it is our hope that other organizations can build on our experiences, benefit from our mistakes, share in our triumphs, and create their own success stories.

The Vision of Cultural Change at the Needmore Road Plant by Our Plant Manager

I think it started—
- When we decided what we stood for.
- When we agreed to include our total work force in decisions affecting our future.
- When we decided to quit copying other systems, other methods, and other ideas.
- When we quit looking for excuses to explain the successes of our competition.
- When we looked at ourselves and decided it was time to evaluate our purpose for existence.
- When we started listening closely to our customers rather than short term bottom line managers.
- When we told the world we were proud of our heritage . . . yet we were willing to change.
- When we told of our strengths and singleness of purpose.
- When we made component plant and vertical integration "bashing" a very unpopular sport of the news media.
- When we decided to show the world we make the best damn components at the right cost and quality.
- When we showed to all, we had a dedicated work force . . . that knew the shared vision and mission of the Needmore Road Plant of Delco Moraine NDH.
- When we honestly evaluated ourselves and looked for reasons to get involved.
- When all our people joined forces to overwhelm our competitors.
- When it became fun to come to work.
- When it became possible for all of us, elected union representatives, managers and the entire work force, to take the risks that were necessary as dictated by the times.

And finally . . .

We are the best and will remain so with this kind of enthusiastic work force. We will remain a strong, viable components manufacturer and will enhance our chances for future growth because of this kind of vision by our total work force.

Section I

Soft-Side Activities

Chapter 1

INITIAL ACTIVITIES

When our participative efforts began five years ago, our approach was not unlike past efforts. We were anxious to *"get started"* in a process that although somewhat mandated by upper management, held promise of improved relationships and performances in the workplace.

With an agreement between the UAW and GM on the value of such efforts and that these efforts should be jointly implemented, we began what turned out to be a necessary change effort laden with successes, failures, frustrations, mistrust, and the frequent questions of *"Is it worth it?"* and *"Who's in charge?"*

Our focus in the beginning was to establish employee participation groups that were given problem-solving and meeting skills that would allow them to solve work-related problems.

These activities were spearheaded by union and management coordinators who were given the responsibility of presenting orientations to the workforce, conducting team training, and leading facilitator skills workshops. It should be noted that during the orientation, it was always made clear that participation by anyone, union or management, was voluntary.

Over 800 employees (about 20% of the workforce) were trained and approximately 100 Employee Participation Groups (EPG's) were formed, primarily in the manufacturing areas. Attendees at these train-ing efforts were primarily hourly rate employees and first line supervisors. Occasionally we had general supervisors attend. On less frequent occasions, we had superintendents participate. As the employee teams came on stream, the coordinators were responsible for their "health" and operation.

The Grenade Lobbing Stages

As time passed, we began to realize that we had put together a program and a process with the best intentions, but that two major stumbling blocks were beginning to surface.

First, the employees and the managers were both looking at this adventure in Participative Management as a significant failure. Even though they both recognized there were some successes and growth along the way, they were viewing it from two different perspectives.

From the management side, we were hearing:
- We are losing production by allowing our people to meet one hour per week, and we are forced to work overtime to make it up.
- We need more *"bang"* for our bucks. We are not seeing any real savings for our investment in this process.
- We have turned the *"asylum over to the inmates."* Participation has turned to permissiveness.
- Where are the team minutes? We need to know what they are doing. Don't *they* trust *us*?
- Teams are goofing off, reading newspapers, playing games, and not getting any results.
- Teams are dying, quitting, and losing interest.
- Teams need to work on more meaningful projects. (Not floorboards, water fountains, break areas, fans, etc.)
- What are *"they"* working on? *"They"* are not telling us. *"They"* are not communicating.

From the employees side we were hearing:
- We want to make a contribution but we need help.
- We are looking for projects but no one from management is offering ideas.
- We are asking for more knowledge about the business (how is it run, what are the objectives, etc.) but with little or no feedback.
- Water fountains are getting boring.
- We have submitted some good ideas, but those that have been approved seem to be *"stonewalled."*
- We are looking for management visibility and support.

Essentially each side was saying the same thing but from a different perspective, and they were saying them to us, as coordinators, but not to each other, at least not on a formalized basis.

Second, in the midst of all this verbiage and discontent (with both sides ready to forfeit or even fight) we found ourselves as coordinators being the *"sole owners"* of the process (or what was left of it).

What went wrong and, more importantly where did we go from here? Looking back on our experiences and the development of the process, we as coordinators began to realize that the structure we had hurriedly established to introduce participative management to our division, had lead us into an ownership trap and that anything of importance should come down through the mainstream of the organizational structure.

ILLUSTRATION A

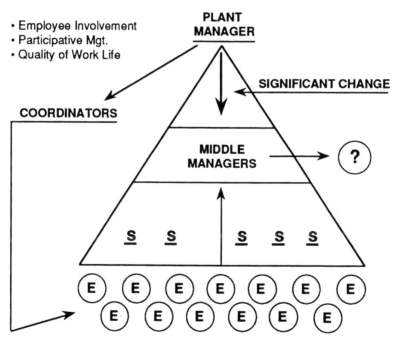

There was no shared vision from bottom to top and how it related specifically to each manager's role.

As shown in Illustration "A", Our Plant Manager along with Union Leadership had appointed union and management coordinators *outside* the mainstream of the organization to learn all they could about the process and pass it on to the organization, particularly to the manufacturing work force.

As a result, several problems surfaced in the initial development of our process.

By focusing our training on the hourly workforce, we ignored a significant number of union leaders and middle managers who were left out of the process. These folks who were by-passed were confused as to which direction the "change process" was working. They saw no short or long term benefits of this change effort.

The typical manager saw proble- solving teams meeting once per week but solving nothing and they were looking to the coordinators to *"fix"* the team. The team members were trained in interpersonal skills and problem-solving skills but knew nothing about the basic issues of running the business such as department goals, burden and labor budgets, product costs, scrap costs, cost reduction goals, schedules vs capacity, competition, market share and costs, quality trends, etc.

There were mixed expectations of the *"New Program"* and no real integrated plans with specific objectives and measurement criteria.

Additionally, we saw a lot of *"Creative Avoidance"* toward a process that had no obvious answers to the question, *"What's in it for me?"* Several managers gave us a sense of abdication when we were frequently asked the question, *"How are 'your' teams doing?"* or more blatant questions such as, *"When are you you going to go back to work?"* or *"When are you going to do real work?"* which gave a not-so-subtle message that our efforts were of questionable value. Managers were looking at the process and the coordinators as a failure and not as a first step in changing the culture of Delco Moraine NDH. They saw the coordinators as a significant expense they could live without.

From the coordinators' point of view, they had not necessarily asked for this job, but they were given the responsibility and a message to deliver—a message that was formulated and agreed upon by the International Union and GM Leadership. They were now in the position of not only delivering the message, but defending it as well.

That all-important message was PARTICIPATION and the implementation was multi-faceted: move the decision-making process to the lowest levels possible, improve the Q.W.L. of all employees, deal with the human side of the organization, learn how to respond to change, develop trust, and improve working relationships that would in time (as a by-product), give us *world-class* quality and productivity levels.

This knowledge imbalance combined with the lack of top down organizational support virtually lead to the demise of 100 Employee

Participation Groups. A few teams were still functioning, but only on a limited basis.

It became fully evident that we must look for ways to shift ownership of the process to joint Management and Union Leadership, especially if we agreed that the concept of Participative Management and its benefits were to be a part of Delco Moraine NDH's operating philosophy and long range change efforts. We needed to *create a culture* where we *believed* that jointly our people could solve their own problems and that they would accept the challenges of being responsible for their own performance.

Chapter 2

MAINSTREAMING THE PARTICIPATIVE PROCESS

One of the simplest models of change effort centers around three basic steps: Awareness—Dissatisfaction—Change, which says that with awareness comes dissatisfaction and with this dissatisfaction will come change.

I think most people even remotely connected to the automotive industry will agree that awareness has been thrust upon us in a "no holds barred" competitive struggle.

Even so, until a level of dissatisfaction is created that will compel managers, hourly workers and union leadership to invest their time and energy to carry through a change effort policy, we will see no real ongoing self-sustaining gains. Without a lot of "grunt work" at the grass roots level, with a de-emphasis on "who gets the credit", we will generally experience fragmented efforts with pockets of successful ventures but no overall permeation of the organization and its workforce.

In the previous chapter, we detailed our initial efforts, frustrations, and lessons. The key issue was that the union and management coordinators were looking at the last dying gasps of a process designed to establish values so needed in our workplace. Without ownership in the mainstream of the organization, the needs of both sides could not be discussed jointly and dealt with. The content issues could not be resolved and relationships could not be established by working through trust barriers.

The Steering Committee

During the 1984 UAW-GM negotiations, the stage was set for a more comprehensive set of guidelines that would enable each plant location to successfully develop a truly *joint participation* process. Included in these guidelines were statements on (1) the values and ethics inherent in any successful process, (2) guidelines for the makeup of a quality-of-work-life steering committee, and (3) the functions of that committee.

Values and Ethics

- Recognition of the right of workers to participate in decisions affecting their working lives.
- Acknowledgement of the worth of all individuals and their right to be treated with dignity and respect.
- Recognition that workers are a valuable resource, in mind as well as body.
- Creation of an atmosphere of trust and openness.
- Encouragement of individuals to maximize their human potential.
- Provisions for individual growth and development.

Guidelines for the Makeup of a Steering Committee

- A coordinating body to guide the process, not a problem solving group.
- Membership limited to six to twelve individuals.
- Appointment of positions equally shared by Union and Management.
- Selection criteria: ability to work with others, credibility with both groups, understanding of their organization, and commitment to quality-of-work-life goals.

Steering Committee Functions

Establish short and long term goals to achieve through the Q.W.L. **process**. The Q.W.L. **process** is defined as:
- A strategy to achieve business objectives.
- A philosophy of work.
- A labor-management partnership.
- Employee involvement in job related problem solving and decision making.
- Joint efforts to improve organizational efficiency, job security, and the quality of people's work experiences.
- A work group concept for now and the future.

Develop and monitor budget

- Recognize limitations of budget.
- Determine the best use of available funds.
- Identify future needs.
- Define the budget for the following year.

Develop and maintain communication systems

- Between teams.
- Between shifts.
- To upper management and union leadership.

Analysis of the organization

- Is the process making a difference?
- Are there teams that need help?
- How are we doing with respect to our goals?

Establish and maintain an implementation plan such as:

- All decisions are joint.
- Decisions by *consensus*.
- Leadership is shared in all problem solving groups.
- Awareness for everyone in the plant.
- Provide environment for maximum participation.

Ensure separation of collective bargaining process and Q.W.L.

- What teams can/cannot work on.

Identify training needs such as:

- Awareness
- Communication skills
- Group development
- Presentation skills
- Meeting skills

In order to pick up the pieces and build on some common understanding developed during our past efforts, we proposed to the Joint Local Committee (Plant Managers, Union President and Chairman of the Shop Committee) that we have an eight-hour workshop designed around the formation of steering committees for each plant and the facilities support group. This was no small undertaking since it involved approximately 250 hourly and salaried employees. The union leadership readily agreed but the Plant Managers were somewhat hesitant (based on past experiences) and understandably so.

Our Plant Manager made it clear that he expected to come away with *concrete plans* for steering committee activity. We carried through with the workshop and the steering committee process began.

Shown in Illustrations B and C are the before and after organization structures with the primary focus of ownership shifting from the coordinators to the Joint Local Committee and the respective plant steering committees.

ILLUSTRATION B

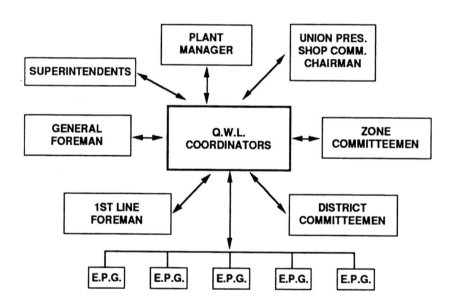

10 - Soft-Side Activities

ILLUSTRATION C

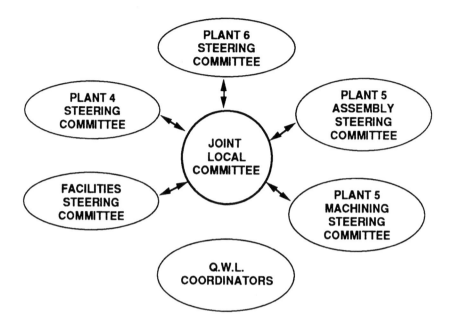

Some of the first questions from the newly formed steering committees were how much power do we really have and to whom do we report? My question to them was, "How much do you want?" The answers to their questions and mine were to come with time.

As roles and responsibilities on both sides of the organization were being redefined, the process and concept of "jointness" as it applied to divisional change efforts became a critical issue. Some of the key points identified were:
- What change efforts should be addressed jointly?
- At what point in time should change efforts become jointly considered?
- What should be the lines of communication for awareness, input, and approval?
- Who would be the key players in the decision making process?
- Who could initiate change efforts?

Because of these and many other concerns, our steering committees, along with union and management leadership, set up a one day conference to share concerns, clarify objectives, review and adopt a change proposal model (see Illustration D). This model has now become an important part of our change effort activities at the plant level.

ILLUSTRATION D

MODEL*

Change Proposal:

- Generate Idea.
- Take to Steering Committee.
- Hold meetings with union, management and hourly employees to discuss barriers
- If changes in classification or rates are a possibility, consult divisional labor relations.
- Design plan.
- Determine potential impact on contract, policy, and management systems; contact concerned parties.
- Check design to be sure barriers are addressed.
- Review again with steering committee.
- Present to jobs sub-committee.
- Present to shop committee.
- Develop implementation plan.
- Implement.

Change Initiatives:

- Hourly Employee
- Manufacturing Management
- Organizational Development Coordinators
- Union Representatives
- Human Resource Coordinators
- Steering Committees

Steps can be simultaneous or sequential.

Chapter 3

PARTICIPATIVE vs PERMISSIVE

I did not have the opportunity of being a part of the initial change effort process, but I suspect my approach would not have been significantly different. Entering the process two years after the fact, opens up opportunities for *"Monday morning quarterbacking"* which has no real value, except to establish a base upon which to build.

After the demise of approximately 100 employee participation groups, there was much soul-searching as to the value of the process and why it didn't get us what we wanted. One of the battle cries we heard when much of the change process was coming apart was, *"We have been permissive and not participative."*

When we had the opportunity to mainstream the process through steering committees and deal with long term issues on a joint basis, we experienced several events which have reinforced our desire and willingness to involve our people more than ever before.

After serving two and half years as a quality-of-work-life coordinator and helping to implement the joint steering committees, I was transferred to manufacturing as a General Supervisor over an assembly area with 275 people and eight supervisors, covering a two shift operation.

Soon after taking this assignment I found myself being asked on numerous occasions to resolve purchased parts quality problems from several different employees. In this area fifty percent of the product cost is in purchased parts which at that time came from 35 to 40 different suppliers. As a result I asked for volunteers to serve on a supplier quality team which was made up of one employee from each production area on both shifts (seven in all).

At our first meeting we established the following guidelines:
- Every member was to receive a complete listing of all suppliers with a telephone number and a contact name.
- Any member could use my phone to call any supplier at any time to report a quality problem.

- Each shift would keep a log book on their contacts and subsequent resolutions.
- They would meet every two weeks to share their results between shifts and with me (at the beginning of the second shift or at the end of the first shift).

Three days later I received a call from our purchasing department asking if I knew one of my employees, Margaret Eaton, was making phone calls to suppliers in New Jersey. I stated that I was not aware but that I believed what they were saying. They went on to say that she was demanding that the supplier have a representative at our place by the next day to resolve a clip problem. I stated, *"I believe that too."* The buyer went on to say, *"Who is giving her permission to do this?"* I stated that I was. His reply was, *"But you can't do that."* *"Why not?"* I asked. *"It's not the proper procedure. Besides that, they may do something wrong that may cause us some problems with our supplier."* (Proper procedure involved a lot of paperwork and 10 to 15 days response time.) The representative showed up the next day and Margaret resolved her problem.

With several calls from different buyers about what was going on, we decided to ask all the buyers to meet with our supplier quality team and let them explain what they were trying to accomplish. Subsequently, we met the buyers in the purchasing conference room for a two hour conference that, on occasion, got a little *"testy"*, but nevertheless brought some understanding as to what the team was trying to accomplish — quicker response, accountability, understanding of our manufacturing process, and resolution of quality problems before the supplier ran additional parts with the same defect.

The reaction from our suppliers was outstanding in three significant ways. First, the response time was cut to a maximum of two days, but generally one day has been the norm. Second, they have expressed their thanks for an opportunity to correct problems in a timely manner. And third, these issues have been dealt with by the employees doing the job. Some suppliers have also brought their employees to our plant to meet with our employees and tour our facilities.

About the same time I received the initial call from our purchasing department, I got a call from one of our plant security people asking, *"Who is Kay Hoover?"* I stated that she worked for us on number five assembly line. He said *"Well, I have two salesmen up here to see her!"* As I said, *"OK, I'll send her right up,"* he began to stutter and I hung up! And Kay went to see the salesmen!

As with the buyers, the salesmen calling on hourly rate employees was different. This was change. It was not all that comfortable. Was it permissive? No! Was it participative? Yes! Was it working? Yes! Lots of quality problems have been fixed since then and our people have a large collection of identified/corrected defects they proudly display as targets of their efforts.

During the past union election, the leadership at the top changed hands. As with most change there were rumors. Specifically in this case, there were rumors that the new top leaders were not favorable to the participative activities currently in place. With this in mind, some of our employees came to my office and asked if they could invite these new union leaders to the department and walk them through the change efforts they were involved in and reinforce their desire to continue. A four hour "show and tell", completely organized and carried out by several hourly employees, was followed by excellent support and positive feedback from the new union leadership resulting in a highly effective assimilation process. Was this permissive? I think not! Participative? You make the call!

Other By-Products of the Participative Process

After the success of the Supplier Team, other needs became apparent and resulted in numerous activities as outlined below.

Customer Quality Teams—These teams were structured somewhat the same as the supplier quality team except that they dealt with the customer, his complaints, and our finished products. These teams have visited assembly plants and car dealerships, and have designed a *"pride"* label they attach to finished parts going to their customers. (See Illustration E)

Business Team—This group has one representative from each line, plus their supervisor. Primary interest centers around what kinds of things go into the running of a business. They have had speakers from such areas as marketing, product engineering, purchasing, new product teams, strategic business units, the union president, and the plant comptroller. Their goal is to take this information back to their respective groups thereby building a knowledge base that may in time allow them to make viable business decisions with respect to their product line.

Resource Center—This once vacant office was reworked and is now dedicated to any information regarding the product we produce including prints, model cutaways, pictures, competitor's parts, marketing brochures, training manuals, cost of all parts going into our products, current trade magazines, future plans, quality team log books, etc. It has also turned out to be a good place for *"show and tell"* during V.I.P. tours.

Training Opportunities—In excess of $100,000 was allocated for various training functions by the UAW Joint Training Fund based on needs identified in the area.

Experimental Production Units—Two, five-to-seven man production units commonly called *"U-Cells"* (as opposed to our 35 to 40 person assembly lines) were designed as joint effort to address flexibility, schedule performance, quality, and quality-of-work-life.

Management by Sight—Implementation of projects such as reduction of finished piston sub-assemblies from 175,000 pieces down to 20,000 pieces ahead of final assembly lines opened up enough area to install one of the *"U-Cell"* areas.

Routine Supplier Visits—A quality representative from Plastic Molding Corporation, our single supplier of pistons, visits with our people once each week to review quality levels and any significant problems we may have experienced with his product. He has even participated in a couple of the V.I.P. tours with our employees.

V.I.P. Tours—The most rewarding by-product of the joint process was exemplified during one of our high level V.I.P. tours. (Generally, many, if not all, of our divisional staff people become part of these highly structured *"events."*) Typical of most of the V.I.P. tours, this one had a very tight timetable and embraced the *"show must go on"* attitude. One of the stops was at our *resource center* with a presentation and discussion by four of our employees. As I looked into the resource center, I suddenly realized that here were four of our people having a full-blown conversation with a vice-president, a general manager, and plant manager about taking responsibility for themselves plus the performance of their department — and they had been at it for over 30 minutes! Outside, the staff was getting impatient and I was getting questions like *"What's going on in there?"*, *"We are behind schedule, what can you do to move things along?"*, *"How are we going to finish in time?"*, etc. My only thought was that our grass roots people are making a commitment and they have someone willing to listen. And my only comment was, *"They have something to talk about!"* For years I have made the presentations and I was expected to say all the good things and put our best foot forward. Now it's their turn and they welcomed the opportunity!

ILLUSTRATION E

PACKED WITH

PRIDE

BY DEPT. 513 - DELCO MORAINE
DAYTON, OHIO
IF THESE PARTS DO NOT MEET
YOUR REQUIREMENTS, PLEASE CALL
(CENTREX) 8-275-5242 - C. BIRKHOLZ

    or M. HUTCHISON — 1st
    or J. KEATON — 1st
    or W. FULLER — 2nd

Chapter 4

GRASS ROOTS OBSERVATION OF CHANGE

Processes—Roles—Tools

> *"If you can see in any situation only what everybody else can see, you can be said to be so much a representative of your culture that you are a victim of it." (S.I. Hayakawa)*

At the heart of the grass roots change efforts is the process by which such changes are brought about. Why are some changes successful but seemingly short lived? Why do some receive lots of fanfare but never go beyond talk? Is the process one of training the experts to *"fix"* them? (Them being the folks responsible for producing the product.) Is the process one of managers having the ability of using the key words and the key phrases when attending strategy meetings and/or conducting the many red carpet tours for our customers, the GM corporate people, or other divisional people looking for a new idea that just might work back at their home bases? Is it a process where we as managers offer new concepts to our people and when they fail, we have a *"convenient"* out which proves the people aren't ready for responsibility or more blatantly, *"I tried, but it really doesn't work!"*

In our experiences we have seen these and many other process variations (meant to address corporate mandates), centered around well intentioned efforts, to meet the ever present competitive pressures in the market place. Despite these efforts to satisfy the corporate objectives, we continue to experience results, that are slow in coming, less than satisfying, and certainly less than the market is going to accept.

If we want our supervisors, general supervisors and superintendents to pursue a course of innovation, creativity, participative management and risk taking, and at the same time involve the union leadership as a partner,

I feel there are some key process issues that must be addressed. In addressing these issues, we can move from a short term, activity-oriented focus to a long term process that will build on itself and not be dependent on one or two *change agents* trying to continually revive *"their"* process or teams along the way.

Among the key issues is *"enabling the workforce."* We are not only talking about the hourly workforce but all of the managerial personnel and the union leadership. All of these groups have talked about change and the need for it. They have experiences they can share both good and bad. On different occasions each *"side"* sees themselves as being more progressive and aggressive than the other resulting in numerous claims and counter-claims and a falling back to *"I remember when"*, and *"I'm not sure who can be trusted,"* and *"Your motivations for change are questionable at best."*

Much of this reaching back (when conflict arises or when major issues are being dealt with) is simply a result of the way we have been trained or conditioned to react in our past relationships. Additionally, many of the new concepts or new approaches we are exposed to, do not match our past experiences, therefore our reactions range from *"I'm not sure"* to *"outright rejection"* because it doesn't fit with what we know to be successful.

My point here is that during any change effort all major parties; the hourly employees, the salary workforce and the union leadership need a grass roots understanding of group dynamics, a definition of their individual role (agreed upon and/or understood by all three parties) and new tools that will empower them to carry out their new roles. My experience has been that employees from all three of these groups are saying *"I want to be a part of this change effort, but where do I start? What can I do? I am just one person! I have never done anything of this nature before."* They understand the need and they understand it is part of the overall competitive issue surrounding component divisions.

Dual Movement of Change

Several years ago I heard the phrase *"dual movement of change"* and at that time the speaker referenced Irving Bluestone as its author. Today this phrase fits a multitude of role changes that are becoming necessary if we are going to be a *pro-active* world class competitor.

In the recent past (in some cases even today) if we were to ask our manufacturing supervisors, general supervisors and superintendents to list the most common things they talk about (to each other) or deal with on a daily or weekly basis, the subjects would have undoubtedly included many of the following topics:

- Production
- Quality ratings
- Maintenance
- Attendance
- Manpower
- Schedule performance
- Scrap pieces and dollars
- Safety
- Discipline
- Housekeeping
- Grievances
- Labor efficiency

As a general supervisor, many of these functions were my primary focus whether I was talking to my boss or my subordinates. Sure these things were important, and I had a very comprehensive goal book in which to record our monthly progress; but something was missing.

Our focus seemed so short term. Most of our time was dedicated to getting through the day or the week and *"getting the numbers."* If 90% of our time was being spent on these issues, then who was taking care of those things needed to prepare us and our employees for the future? Had we become overpaid baby-sitters who were about to become obsolete in a changing market we knew little or nothing about? Were our decisions being based primarily on internal measurements leading us down that infamous primrose path, oblivious to the real time measurements of the market place?

The answers were "yes" and it became somewhat obvious that the roles of the supervisors, the employees and the union leadership had to change. Sure we had to maintain all of the short term day-to-day functions as noted earlier, but there had to be quality time spent on some long term building functions and in order to do so, all of our roles were going to change, and so was the use of our time.

The new roles were eventually to be built around such key issues as:

- Job Awareness
- Training Needs
- Customer Needs
- Team Work
- Communication Systems
- Support Systems
- Product Knowledge
- Trust
- Vendor Relationships
- Common Vision
- Resource Availability
- Management Performance

Soft-Side Activities - 21

And this is where the *"fireworks"* began. This is where group dynamics, conflict, politics, one-up-manship, past practices, current agreements, personal preferences, peer pressures, etc. required time, patience and a lot of ground level work with the involvement of all parties.

This is where the *"dual movement of change"* begins to shake out. This is where the *"baby-sitter"* gives up his role and begins spending 30-40-50% of his time addressing the long term building functions. This is where people shift from *"malicious obedience"* or *"tell me exactly what to do"* or *"top down order taking"* to taking responsibility for themselves and to managing performance. This is where the employees begin handling some of the short term maintenance functions (their choice) which allows their supervisor to reach out and deal with the groups long term building needs. Of course this *"dual movement"* becomes delicate and tricky since both the supervisor and worker need an abundance of training to enable them to take on these *new,* and I might add, more fulfilling roles. This movement also finds that some union committeemen are attending steering committee meetings, jobs committee meetings, communication meetings, training sessions, special task force meetings, off-sites, etc. This gives him much more latitude in representing his people. And just what does all this involvement, awareness, conflict, training, role changes, etc. do for the division and its people? Maybe it's just a sense of purpose.

Some time ago I asked our employees at several workshops if they were glad they worked at Delco Moraine NDH. The answer, of course, was an overwhelming *"yes."* And the reasons given were predictable; good wages—best in town, good benefits for family security and good working conditions. But when I asked the question, *"How many of you are proud you work at this division?,"* the response was not a positive one. Aside from some of the ways we had treated each other in the past, they cited comments from their neighbors and from the press centered around quality, price and inflated wages. They also cited the many instances where they personally were dissatisfied with their new cars and the service at new car dealerships.

I then asked them to consider how we could move from being just glad we work here, to being proud we work here? I feel the answer lies somewhere in this *"dual movement of change."* Specifically it is taking responsibility for oneself, giving up babysitting duties, managing performance at the lowest levels, and staying in tune with the real time *measurements* in the marketplace.

Just maybe it could result in a significant cultural change. While sitting in my office one day, someone handed me an advertisement entitled *The Law of the Hog* sponsored by Interact of Santa Ana, California. The article focuses on the interpersonal relationships of employees and supervisors at a plywood mill in a small company town. After Interact consultants had interviewed employees and managers at the plant, they found that when relationships broke down between the two groups there was this practice of *"feeding the hog,"* the hog being a huge machine, designed to chop up wood scraps that could not be made into plywood. Only in this case the hog was being fed good pieces of veneer. Why? To get back at the supervisors by destroying profits. How many of us have fed the hog in the past? Not just in manufacturing but in other parts of the organization?

I shared this story with some of my people in a workshop where our emphasis was on cultural change in the workplace. When I had finished one of our employees raised her hand and asked *"Can I tell you some of the ways we have fed the hog?"* My answer, *"I don't mind if you don't!"* As the employees began relating the many ways they and their peers had fed the hog, the balance of the workshop became an interesting group to observe. Once they got past the fear of *"telling on themselves,"* the learning experience was invaluable. So too was the realization that our many joint change efforts at Delco Moraine NDH have reduced the desire to feed the hog. Hopefully we can get him on the endangered species list.

Soft-Side Activities - 23

Reaching Back

> *"It's not so much that we're afraid of change, or so in love with the old ways, but it's that place in between we fear...it's like being in between trapezes. It's "Linus" when his blanket is in the dryer. There's nothing to hold on to." (M. Ferguson)*

Reversing from a *"top-down order giving"* style of management (where good news goes up and bad news comes down) would seem to be a breath of fresh air for all employees whether management, hourly or union leadership. Not so! The transition route is unwieldly, unknown and at best fraught with the values of old versus new. One example that keeps coming to the forefront in our supervisors' meetings accentuates this struggle. Some of our supervisors have welcomed the new opportunities made available through a growing and enhancing type of atmosphere and have made some real significant contributions through their willingness to take a risk, give their people an opportunity to take responsibility for themselves and take full advantage of the opportunity to broaden their skills. In the midst of these successes we still have other supervisors in the *"yes but..."* syndrome.

Yes, but... we are losing control. Yes, but... we are being permissive and not participative. Yes, but... those people (hourly employees) will never take responsibility for themselves no matter what you do to help. Yes, but... I am not giving up my right to supervise. Yes, but... what about our company policies, shop rules and our demand settlements?

We have spent years focusing on the boss as the one to plan, organize and control and the employee has carried out the assignment or tasks. *We* do the thinking and *you* do the work. This thought process has been perpetuated by signs, booklets, slide presentations, safety handouts, etc. that said, *"Got a problem? See your supervisor."* What kind of culture did it foster?

- The supervisor carried the full responsibility of solving problems which at best is very inefficient.
- The hourly employee came to work, did the task assigned him, and clocked out with no thought given to his job until the next day—a splendid example of non-ownership!
- The supervisor's list of things to do grew longer and longer.
- *"You get me good parts and keep the equipment running and I'll get*

the production for you!"—a good way to keep the *"boss"* on the defensive.
- Our side and your side was easy to maintain with distrust as the dividing force in keeping us miles apart even though our long term goals were by necessity the same.
- The goals, vision, mission, customer needs and identity seemed always too muddled in a strategy of one-up-manship.

Is this what we want to return to? I think not!

Nevertheless, getting there *ain't easy*. The only tools we have in our possession are those learned under the old order and it's easy to reach back and grab the hammer. It's comfortable. It seems like the right thing to do. Learning new ways of doing things, teaching employees new ways of doing things, maintaining the productivity goals, planning for the future and not just getting through the day is hard work. It is transitional. It is different. It's loaded with "trust the process" lingo, and it does not always feel right. And just maybe, if I hold out long enough, this program will soon pass like all those before!

I think this is time for a note of caution. There are many pressures that bear on a person in any group, whether it be an hourly employee or a member of supervision or union leadership that steps out with a willingness to change, take a risk and do something different. He/she can always expect to take some hits from his/her peer group; it goes with the territory.

At the other end of the spectrum there are also rumblings from the troops about the *"yes, but . . ."* supervisors who are not handling the transition as readily as some of their peers. The impatient messages to me are: you have given them enough time; make it mandatory; they've always used the hammer and they are not going to change; and what are you going to do about it? Obviously this is where developmental needs begin to surface and should be dealt with on an individual basis. It sounds simple, but the general supervisor's ability to explore and identify such developmental needs for these new supervisory roles may stifle the whole process. This ability stems from a lack of skills . . . not a lack of desire. And so it goes on up the ladder. And this is the challenge we all face. How do we simultaneously train each level for the new order of things, keep the business afloat and deal with all of the turmoil created by the transitional change efforts designed to reach a desired future state? Definitely not by reaching back!

Adults—Parents—Children

From our birth to the age of five or six years of age our parents were our great protectors. They fed us, clothed us and concerned themselves with our health and safety. They told us what to do, when to do it, and how to do it. There were many things to learn and we learned quickly.

As we began our school experiences, we found ourselves with a teacher who replaced our parents for a big portion of the day. We found out early on that the teacher would be telling us what to do, when to do it, and how to do it.

As we began our work experience, we found ourselves with a boss who replaced our parents and teachers for a big portion of the day. We found that our bosses would be telling us what to do, when to do it, and how to do it!

As I related this concept to some of our employees in a workshop someone raised their hand and said, "You forgot one other step in the process, my drill sergeant." Of course this concept is oversimplified, but we have allowed this parent-child relationship to exist and function in our manufacturing culture far too long.

We have had numerous discussions with our people on how the child (employee) can make the parent (supervisor) act dumb, such as being late for work, openly ignoring safety rules, running poor quality, etc. We ask our folks, *"Is this really the way you want to use your supervisor; telling you when you're late, when to put a machine guard up or down, when to wear safety glasses, or check your parts?"* Or would a better approach be to take responsibility for your own actions, thus allowing your supervisor to dedicate a significant portion of his/her time to non-traditional activities such as:

- Visiting our customers and suppliers, along with employee representatives, in order to improve quality and customer relations.
- Developing training programs for his people in order to raise their skill levels.
- Conducting communications meetings focused on managing your own performance.

We have also talked about the ways a parent (supervisor) can make the child (employee) act dumb. They are numerous, and mostly centered around trust. Of course parents know there are many reasons why a child cannot be trusted!

This dilemma is reflected in a short quote from a poem we have used in our Delco Moraine NDH workshops during the past four years. (Author unknown)

What is it about that entrance way
Those gates to the plant?
Is it the guards, the showing of your badge, the smell?
Is there some invisible eye that pierces
you through and transforms your being?
Some aura or ether that brain and spirit washes
you and commands,
"for eight hours you shall be different."
What is it that instantaneously makes a child out of a man?

Our lessons here beg the question of why can't we elevate our interpersonal relationships from the parent-child level to an adult–adult level? What about taking on new rolls, ownership and responsibility for ourselves?

In order to break out of this relationship each side must give the other room to change, to experiment, to make some mistakes. Attempting to reach the adult–adult relationships requires working through a lot of history loaded with distrust, scars, wounds, and ownership problems. And, oh yes, there will be some who will abuse new found freedoms. They will no doubt get a failing grade. They will get lots of attention but please don't make any more new rules. The other 90-95 percent will be with you as adults.

Designed to Fly

As a kid, I had this off-the-wall dream that someday I was going to learn how to fly an airplane. Because of the expense involved, this dream was easily set aside for some future date. As an adult this dream became somewhat of a reality when, on an impulse, I stopped at our local airport and talked to the fixed based operator about his five dollar introductory offer. Within ten minutes he had introduced me to one of his instructors, and we were soon busy doing a visual check of one of the aircraft. Within the hour I had my half-hour introductory flight, purchased and filled out a log book, and had made an appointment for my next flight and instructions. I was an easy sell and I was having fun!

During the early stages of my dual instructions I seemed to have trouble keeping the wings level and the nose of the plane at the proper attitude so that it would neither gain nor lose altitude. After experiencing this several times my instructor began this lecture (which I suspect he had delivered on many occasions in the past and at just the right time).

"Charlie, I would like to give you some information about this aircraft. It was designed by Cessna Aircraft company engineers to fly. It was built by Cessna aircraft manufacturing people to fly. It is certified by the FAA that it is airworthy and will fly. Now look at your left hand. Your knuckles are white from holding on to the yoke so tight. You are so concerned about keeping the nose up and the wings level that you will not let the plane fly itself. Relax! Turn loose! Cradle the yoke in the palm of your hand. Watch the plane fly itself. Watch the horizon. Watch the instruments. Listen to your engine. Set your trim controls and the plane will fly. If at times you need to make a mid-course correction, then do so. But don't over-control."

It just may be that we have organizations wanting to fly; individuals that want to innovate, take risks, and contribute; systems that are designed to give us that competitive edge but our *"white knuckle"* approach is giving us some unwanted and unusual attitudes and experiences. Our high need for control and the resulting reactions are not giving us the expected results, and we are not sure why.

Our challenge (as additional experience and results from participative involvement activities are beginning to support) is to *turn the asylum over to the inmates* as one consultant so aptly stated it— a phrase that does not overstate the fear in some managers' minds. It is a fear that we must overcome, a fear that we are overcoming for a lot of reasons including that of necessity. As Maryann Keller, auto analyst for Furman, Seix, Mager, Dietz, and Birney states, *"I always felt that components divisions could be a gold mine for General Motors, but were just never properly run. There's no place else in the world where there is that much manufacturing know how.*

"When it comes to understanding the needs of a company and wanting to change, the hourly worker deserves a gold star. I'm not sure that story's ever been told. The hourly worker has been asked to change how he works, he's been asked to change what he does, he's been asked to change where he does it, and they've accepted it. It is the hourly workers on the shop floor who first feel the pain of corporate failure. It is they (rather than the company's top management) who feel production cuts from excess inventory. It is they who forego profit-sharing checks when profits don't exceed a set level, while salaried employees continue to earn bonuses for individual efforts. I don't think the hourly workforce at General Motors lives in a dream world; they have been educated the hard way. They're just a tremendous asset to the company, and an unheralded asset in my opinion." [The *Dayton Daily News; "The New GM"*; January 24-25, 1988. Allen Roberts, Business Writer.]

It just may be that we have an organization that wants to fly and people that will give us that competitive edge. Let's set the course!

Roasted Duck

While attending the 1987 International Association of Quality Circles Annual Spring Conference, I had the opportunity of hearing Mr. Lawrence Miller speak at the opening session with a focus on quality corporate cultures. He began his speech by asking an unusual question. *"How many in this audience remember the 'Lone Ranger' of western fame? The man that rode a white horse, wore a mask, and carried silver bullets?"* After several hundred of us raised our hands admitting we were old enough to remember, he went on to remind us how the drama and the plots were generally played out. Typically there was a not-too-smart rancher with a beautiful daughter and he had a problem. He either had his water rights cut off, his cattle were stolen, or his mortgage was being foreclosed and he needed help. Naturally in each episode our hero would ride in on his white horse and rescue the rancher. After all the wrongdoing was made right, he would ride off into the distance and someone would always say *"Who was that masked man?"* He went on to say those movies were fun and entertaining, but they were a myth. They were a big hit but they were not real. And so it is in today's corporate business world. If we expect someone to ride in and rescue us, we had better think again!

Later that week I attended a session by Dave Richey which began with a transparency that read: *"A starving man waits a long time for a roasted duck to fly into his mouth."* After seeing this quote I remember little else about his presentation. What he was saying and what Lawrence Miller was saying were right on target with respect to our competitive position as a components division in the GM structure.

If we, as a division (hourly, salary, and union leadership), were going to wait for a masked man from corporate headquarters to ride in on his white horse and rescue us, as a brake division, then we still believe in myths and our survival is not only suspect but highly questionable in today's market. Additionally it's easy to recognize that a starving man will not wait a long time for a roasted duck to fly into his mouth—he will wait forever!

This *"we must help ourselves"* mind-set was significantly reinforced during one of our many red carpet tours at Delco Moraine NDH. One of our G.M. Vice Presidents and several of our hourly employees from the power brake section were gathered in the department resource center discussing the participative activities and changes in which they were currently involved. The discussion was abruptly changed by the Vice President with questions such as: *"I see your enthusiasm, but what about the rest of the folks in the department?"* *"What percent of the workforce is really involved?"* *"Do they really feel like you do?"* *"Are they as concerned as you?"* Pointed questions that alluded to the underlying message, *"What are you doing to help yourselves?"* The next day one of these employees shared this experience at his line communication team meeting (approximately thirty-five people).

The first question out of the group was, *"What did you say?"* *"Did you lie?"* At that point I asked him to hold his answers until I asked the group a couple of questions. The two questions were:

(1) *"How would you folks answer these questions?"* and—
(2) *"Who wants to make a presentation on the next red carpet tour?"*

Needless to say we had a good discussion and the next red carpet tour turned out to be our new G.M. President, Robert Stemple.

Beyond all that has been said here is the point that a significant *cultural change* is necessary in order to compete with the best. Ownership, commitment and involvement from all employees may not be realistic, but I am willing to bet those divisions that make the change will end up with the roasted duck and the silver bullets. As Blair Thompson has stated, "We can't guarantee any business for Dayto*n that their people don't earn. They'll do as well or as poorly as they want to do. And I happen to think they'll do well.*"

Chapter 5

"A TASTE OF SUCCESS"

One of my primary concerns when moving from my role as a Q.W.L. coordinator (part time facilitator, trainer and promoter of participative management) to the mainstream of our manufacturing operations as a general supervisor, was that once we personally started a full, all-out change effort we needed the license to carry it to completion.

Once people experience the impact of their constructive efforts and the ownership that goes with it, we are not at liberty to turn back the clock and repossess that new found experience without a lot of grief and a cry of "foul."

I shared these feelings with my manufacturing superintendent as I came on board as part of his supervisory group. I also expressed my concern that if I ever move from the area for whatever reason, our successor must share the same philosophy or he will be in for the shock of his life.

After 18 months and many successes (and some failures) in participative management efforts, centered around an assembly area populated with some 275 employees, I was reassigned to another area with the expressed purpose of implementing more of the same.

Immediately, perceptions and reactions became the order of the day from our work force. Clearly there was a high level of dissatisfaction and the people wanted to be heard. Some of the perceptions and reactions were:

- Our General Supervisor is being moved and the new process is not totally implemented.
- His replacement has been here before, and we know he doesn't agree with the new way of doing things.
- His replacement has had no preparation or training to carry on this process.

- Upper management doesn't care about the new way of doing things or they wouldn't be doing this. The only one that cares has been our General Supervisor and he is being moved.
- A special meeting was scheduled by the Q.W.L. Steering Committee with the Plant Manager, Personnel Director, Committeeman at Large, Superintendent, etc. to present a petition in the form of a letter with 187 signatures asking for reconsideration of the move.

With these reactions and perceptions in mind, our Plant Manager decided to "go to the floor," listen to the people, take some hits, and explain his reasoning behind the changes. After spending an hour on the floor he decided to have a full departmental meeting with each shift, make a statement on his long term objectives, and field questions from the audience. He also asked that I make a statement about the participative process and that the Superintendent and new General Supervisor reinforce their commitment.

The important issue here became the desire of the people to maintain the participative process. They had experienced ownership, buy-in and commitment toward the success of "their" business, i.e., their objectives, their goals, and their competitive position in the market. There had evolved a "critical mass" of employees who knew where the division was trying to go and any threat to their freedom to be a part of it was considered a serious matter.

These perceptions had to be dealt with in a participative way as our Plant Manager stated, "A year or two ago we were looking for ways to be participative—now that we have it we must listen to the people—it can't be one way!"

Section II

Hard-Side Activities

Chapter 6

A KEY TO TECHNICAL CHANGE

With many of the lessons that we experienced from our "soft-side" activities outlined during the initial portion of this book, we felt that we had the needed *support structures* present within our plant to facilitate joint processes that could be focused on the competitive issues facing our division. At the forefront of these support structures were the individual plant Q.W.L Steering Committee and the Sub-Jobs Committee, that were equally populated by members of management and the work force (which generally included the district committeeman). Additionally, we felt there now existed a "critical mass" of people on both sides, that understood the need for change and were willing to take the risk to lead any significant change effort.

Our plant manager stepped out of his comfort zone to initiate a process that would payoff in the future. Even though he was a self-proclaimed "elder statesman" he and his staff, along with our elected union officials, became proactive in an effort to empower other plant personnel to do things differently.

As mentioned, the first portion of this book has provided an insight into what we call *"Soft-Side Activities."* Soft-side activities can include but not be limited to:
- Employee Involvement
- Attitudes
- Cultural Changes
- Training
- Communications
- Trust
- Team Work
- How We Work Together

These soft side activities have provided the support structures to enable us to deal jointly with *"Hard-Side Activities"* which are centered around the structure and technical side of our organization. Examples of these items could be:

- Equipment
- Repair
- P.M.
- Tooling
- Materials
- Product Costs
- Utilization
- Crew Composition

Another view of this subject is detailed in the *three-sided* industrial organization model (See Figure 1, page 39) presented at a Black Lake Leadership Conference.[1]

Items that take place in the STRUCTURE

The structure generally takes care of itself. Without a structure we would not have an organization. The structure seldom changes, but deviates from time to time because of union elections, personnel changes, bargaining, and mangement decisions. Investment is made in the structure through contracts, promotions, expansion, incentives, etc. The structure has rules, regulations, a financial structure, responsibility, and accountability.

Items that take place on the TECHNICAL (Hard) side

Technology is ever changing with new high tech methods and machines, new products, different market demands, engineering changes and improvements, competition, materials, etc.

There seems to be a large investment in technology and at times companies try to "buy" their way to a competitive position. Some individuals think that without technology, we wouldn't have an organization. Putting it simply, technological needs are seldom questioned.

It seems to be common practice in some areas that the hard-side or technical activities take precedence—and often take place first without a lot of thought on how to maintain them. Since the hard-side activities are visible, they can be perceived to be more important at times to show that improvements are being made. The key to becoming a world class supplier is to balance both hard-side and soft-side activities so that they complement one another.

---

[1]*Black Lake Joint Leadership Conference - 1985*

Three-sided Industrial Organization Model

<u>Structure</u>
Management
Union
Contract
Finance
Bargaining
Personnel
Chain of Command
Buildings

<u>Human</u>
Education
Communication
Involvement
Relations
Attitudes
Trust
Respect
Commitment

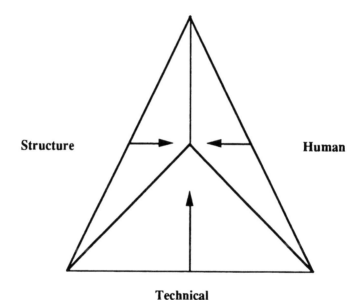

<u>Technical</u>
Machinery
Tooling
Products
Design
Testing
Computers

Figure 1

Hard-Side Activities - 39

When you decide to make a technical change in your environment, you must recognize that the change process has a significant impact on all three sides of the industrial organization. Areas that may need to be addressed are the different needs of plant personnel, training that may or may not be required, trust levels that may have to be fortified/supported, and any additional items that are deemed to be part of the support structure.

Some of the items that take place on the HUMAN (Soft) side

The human side seldom changes because of job security, family, protection, income, retirement, benefits, and contentment with present work status (glad vs proud). The human side is different because of an individual's personality, values, age difference, attitude and behavior, education, self esteem, personal goals, skills and talent, traditions, etc. Typically, the traditional human side has been kept in the dark, is expected to know, do as he/she is told, don't question anything, is not valued, is expected to produce, and is normally blamed for failure. In the past, little investment has been made on the human side of the organization to change the tradition of the work place. Structure and technology have created the only changes with most investment being spent in these areas.

Take a good look at departmental budgets; what percent is targeted for technical activities versus human activities? Structure has not dealt with the individual and the needs for personal growth that will lead to the growth of the entire organization. A constant reminder must be that personal goals must be kept aligned with the plant's goals. They must run parallel with one another or conflict arises. Ownership in the system of change will come with these two areas being satisfied.

As has been previously stated, quality-of-work-life means addressing the human side of the organization. We have learned that employees want to be involved in decisions that affect their jobs. They also want to communicate and know what is happening in their organization. Through our quality-of-work-life efforts, we have found that many positive aspects have surfaced. They include new contract language in our UAW international contract, technical training through the GM/UAW joint training fund, consultants employed where we did not have the soft-side "tools", and most importantly, the necessary financial commitment was made to support what was deemed necessary to go forward.

If you evaluate the three sides of the organizational triangle, there are three distinct viewpoints to consider. When reviewing the structure side, you find that it seldom changes. It may change but would have very little effect on the people. It normally has a financial investment, takes care of itself, and makes decisions for the organization.

When reviewing the technical side, it appears to be ever changing, has heavy investment, its products depend on technology, quality is improved through technology, and the organization is thought to be kept competitive with technological changes.

Finally, the human side consists of people at all levels in the organization. This area involves relationships, attitudes, and trust. It is the human side of the triangle that makes the technical and structure sides of the triangle work. New technology and products change, but people normally are comfortable to stay the *same.* In the past, we have failed to invest properly in the human side of the organization. It will take a significant commitment to play "catch up" in this area of investment.

However, the best training in the world is worthless without the proper attitude. An attitude is based on trust. Trust is earned and can't be imposed or dictated. Trusting can build personal respect and change attitudes. Above all, a positive attitude can create involvement. It's this positive attitude and involvement that combine to enable plant personnel to get involved in a cultural change to make the work place better and regain that

Chapter 7

CONTINUOUS IMPROVEMENT

Delco Moraine NDH produces brake systems for General Motors' cars and trucks. Very little of our sales go outside G.M.. In the past, we had very little competition and the car divisions bought our products without question. We no longer have that luxury. All car divisions are now pursuing the purchase of component parts with the best *QUALITY, DELIVERY,* and *COST.* There are a vast number of competitors, both foreign and domestic, for many of the products that we produce. Our challenges are many, as our competitors are continually improving at an accelerating rate. The competition is not waiting for us to catch up to make it a fair fight. To stay in business and return a profit to our shareholders requires a change in our manufacturing approach.

In the summer of 1986, our plant manager and his staff went off-site to determine the course of action that our plant should take to become a world class manufacturing facility. Many items and concepts were discussed to determine the vision that our plant personnel should have in the future. Since our plant fell within the automotive components group (ACG) of the G.M. corporate structure, our executive vice-president deemed *SYNCHRONOUS MANUFACTURING* as the concept to "get competitive."

This concept is defined as:

> *"The coordination of resources (man/machine/ material) to eliminate waste, resulting from continuous and rapid improvement of the manufacturing process."*

Out of this off-site, the plant manager and his staff came back to the plant with a vision that was put down on paper and became the plant's five-year plan. We started off with a few initial successes that provided some visible hard-side items on the plant floor. We used the elements of synchronous manufacturing to guide us in accomplishing plant changes.

One of our first examples of change was relocating an Acme Chucker and other miscellaneous equipment from two different plants into one centralized area. This was definitely a change in tradition from what we normally did in the plant with regards to rearrangement. This area became known as the "white elephant." We painted it white because we wanted to send a message to the floor that our expectations were that the equipment and work area would be kept clean. This was quite a challenge since most of our plant's Acme Chuckers leaked hydraulic fluid/coolant and in most cases we tolerated the leaks as normal.

At the same time that we moved and consolidated the equipment, we made the decision to go with only one classification of personnel within the working area. Traditionally there had been *three* different classifications that operated this type of equipment. The one-classification concept became known as the "quality operator" concept. Our plant manager and his staff wanted to utilize the concept in this area to evaluate personnel rotating job assignments as well as being responsible for quality within the operator's own work area. Since that time, we have spread the quality operator concept into other areas of the plant.

In the fall of 1986, a decision was made that if synchronous manufacturing were to be the driver for a successful operation, a full-time employee would be required to aid in implementation. I started out as a full-time synchronous manufacturing coordinator in November of 1986. My first assignment was to spread the word to all plant personnel on all three shifts.

I was nominated for the job because I:
- Knew the plant facility
- Had a good solid background in manufacturing and manufacturing engineering
- Had a good relationship with most plant personnel
- Liked to work with people at all levels
- Could take constructive criticism (fairly well)
- Was a risk taker, and not opposed to trying new ideas

Most traditional job assignments that you receive are fairly well defined, with someone having been in that position before. Normally, someone has a fair amount of experience to draw from, and then guides you in your new duties and responsibilities. Since this job was the first of its kind, there weren't any plant personnel that had any practical experience in this area. We were in uncharted waters, so to speak, with the trial-and-error method sometimes being the only way to find out what worked best. Within our plant we have some very capable people that can figure out how to drill a hole in a casting to a very tight tolerance, but when it came to determining how to implement change without too much frustration, we all learned together without any expert help.

Given my assignment of spreading the word to all plant personnel, I had to do a lot of homework and make a few plant visits before I could put down on paper what synchronous manufacturing was and was not. I quickly came to realize that there were many authors out there who had many different thoughts, ideas, and philosophies concerning world class manufacturing, continued improvement, just-in-time concepts, and about anything else that you could imagine to write about. There were also many different philosophies and approaches being tried inside and outside the corporation with varying degrees of success. I decided to go with a basic common sense approach so that the presentation could be understood by all plant personnel, in all areas, on all shifts.

Since I had written the presentation and had made many revisions, it got to the point where I knew the material quite well and was very happy with what I had put together. After the final revision, I took the presentation to the plant manager and his staff for approval. I was pleasantly surprised that there were just a small number of revisions to make after the staff review. During the first few presentations to the plant personnel, it became evident that not everyone shared my viewpoints or even agreed with the new concepts and philosophies being presented. I had to make an honest appraisal of the format and content material of my presentation. Revisions were made where applicable and the presentations continued until *all* plant personnel were exposed to the synchronous manufacturing concepts.

If you look at what we were trying to accomplish, I was about 60% effective in getting the word out. If you look at the goal as being to just give a presentation to a certain number of people, then the goal was 100% effective. My personal goal was to give the presentation, receive feedback, and have everyone depart the session with the same knowledge and enthusiasm that I had for our new manufacturing philosophy.

Such was not the case! I had made notes of all the comments and compiled them for the plant manager and his staff to review. Comments ranged from very negative to very positive. It became evident from the feedback from the plant, that they needed much more information, additional sessions, and questions answered. I then categorized all the questions that I compiled and went back to the plant manager and his staff for discussion. We decided to respond to each question by listing all questions and responses to questions in our plant newsletter. Everyone was not satisfied with the answers, but we did give them a well-deserved response.

Both the hourly rated and salaried employees struggled with some of the new synchronous manufacturing concepts. Some of the first line supervisors found it hard to accept some of the employee involvement items that were beginning to evolve within certain departments. By the same token, some of the hourly rated personnel and union officials had to think about this cultural change and how they fit in.

During the spring of 1987, we had a union election. Both the elected union officials and plant management personnel had worked in the past to support the synchronous manufacturing concept and joint activities in general. After the election, we went through a rebuilding phase on both sides to reestablish and improve relationships to get competitive. I am happy to say that the newly elected union officials decided to work with plant personnel to move forward with current programs. This is not to say that we didn't have problems and numerous discussions within our plant. Human nature dictates different viewpoints and personalities. We took this opportunity to talk about what could be done and how to accomplish changes through our steering committees and sub-jobs committee.

As we progressed through many training sessions given by myself and other plant personnel, it became evident that each plant had areas of activities that helped to change our culture regarding both hard- and soft-side issues. This evidence led me and others to think about various communication options that would enhance what we had already accomplished and further accelerate the change efforts within the plant. A survey was sent out to each plant superintendent for input as to what would be needed, in their opinion, to accomplish further implementation of synchronous manufacturing. After reviewing their comments, a decision was made at the divisional level that a "cascade training system" may enhance the learning process.

A problem that you sometimes encounter on many special assignments is that you become an expert and many rely on you as an expert resource. This is not all bad, but we wanted to be in a position such that more of my knowledge and awareness was shared by many more personnel. The cascade training approach started out at the division's general manager level and "cascaded down" to the plant floor. The general manager trained his staff, which in turn trained their staff. It was hoped that an increasing number of personnel would then become pro-active in the change process. We are still pursuing this training concept within our plant and division.

The philosophy of synchronous manufacturing must be addressed in all organizational disciplines, not just on the manufacturing floor. Customer satisfaction is achieved through quality, price and delivery. Synchronous manufacturing is dependent upon the manufacturing process to produce a good part on demand to achieve customer satisfaction.

One of our component plant evaluation systems that came from our corporate staff was a rating process which would determine the competitive position of our plant, along with all of the other component divisions. This process consisted of rating the products that we produced in our plant against our major competitors in the international market place. Simply stated, each product line that we produced was rated:
- Green
- Yellow
- Red

These ratings are defined as follows:

Green: Producing a component part that is world class in the areas of cost, quality, and delivery.
Yellow: Producing a component part that is world class in one or two of the three areas of cost, quality, and delivery. The other one or two areas will probably be attainable with a reasonable investment.
Red: Producing a product line that does not meet world class standards in any of the three world class areas. Meeting world class standards would probably take an inordinate amount of investment and probably not be achieved by the corporation.

These color code designations are used by the automotive component groups to identify progress being made in their plants. It makes economic sense to invest the corporate dollar in *green* and *yellow* product lines. Having a *green* product also puts component groups in a positive position when pursuing non-allied business.

Some of the issues that were commonly accepted as "hard-side activities", which would help move our products into the green area, were targets for future change efforts. They included:
- Quality, both *from* suppliers and *to* our customers
- Delivery of our products
- Plant costs
- Inventories
- Productivity

Chapter 8

KEY ELEMENTS OF THE SYNCHRONOUS PROCESS

The following implementation elements are being used to guide the continuous improvement process:
- Employee Involvement
- Employee Training
- Man/Machine Effectiveness
- Quality Control
- Setup Reduction
- Preventive Maintenance
- Supplier Relations
- Visual Controls
- Synchronous Scheduling
- Simultaneous Engineering

Employee involvement is listed first and is fundamental for the improvement process. You build your base for change with it.

The existing organization must move from its current state of being non-synchronous to a synchronous state. Implementation strategies and action plans must be in place to create change. (See Figure 2, page 50)

The organization has to be convinced that synchronous manufacturing is the answer to the problem. First we had to create a new structure organized for change. From this structure a climate conducive to synchronous manufacturing objectives had to be developed. In addition, the organization must create the approach that will allow synchronous manufacturing to endure.

To achieve our objective of a synchronous organization required a transition from our current state. We needed to create a vision of what our synchronous plant would look like. Getting to this vision required an organization structured to develop and implement corrective action. The climate that promoted risk-taking and innovation was provided. Emphasis on small, continuous improvement was the approach. Do not try

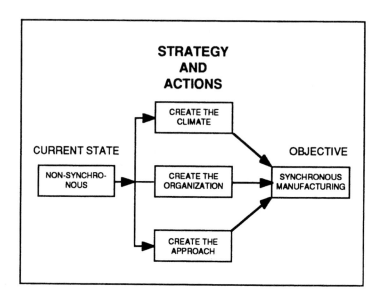

Figure 2

to "eat the elephant." In order to meet the objective, each element required a strategy addressing the organization, the climate, and the approach.

Now, let's take a look at the specifics of each element of synchronous manufacturing.

Employee Involvement

Employee involvement is the key to our success. Breaking down traditional roles that limit participation and involvement in problem solving was essential. An organization that promotes communication based on trust and team work, moved us toward the objective of maximum participation in the improvement process. (See Figure 3, page 51)

Ask yourself these questions:
- How can your plant communications be improved?
- If your plant was your business, how would you make communication more effective in your area?

Specific things that we did:
- Plant newspaper (even though we had a divisional newspaper)
- T.V. (communication) monitors in plant, break areas, cafeteria, conference rooms, etc.
- Special bulletins

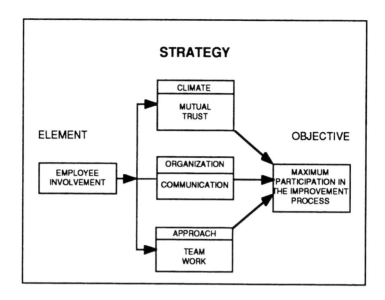

Figure 3

- Communication for Improvement Teams
- Business Teams
- Q.W.L. Steering Committees
- Jobs Committees

The following are some thoughts that Jim Cook, one of our Q.W.L. coordinators, has expressed on employee involvement within our plant.

"Some of us, throughout the organization, have had the misconception that employee involvement only pertains to getting union officials and other hourly people involved in the decisions that management alone has historically made. Others of us have come to the conclusion that it means relinquishing power and allowing unqualified people to run the ship (or turn the asylum over to the inmates). Some of us believe that it is a trend, one that won't work, and if we ignore it long enough it will go away. Some of us also believe that whatever it is, it's difficult to make work."

One thing that is clear to me is that there are good reasons for these misconceptions, but they are indeed misconceptions. Let's take a look at them, one by one.

Why is it that so many of us believe that employee involvement only pertains to union officials and other hourly employees? To answer this, let's take a look at our recent history. In 1973, in the G.M./U.A.W.

contract, the first language dealing with employee involvement, appeared. Not much was done at first, but finally we started what we called an "Employee Participation Group" (E.P.G.) process. The major focus was to get hourly people involved. At one time we had over 100 hourly teams, but we never had more than a few salaried teams. Many of the hourly teams had one or two salaried members, but the vast majority of the members were hourly. Whether or not the E.P.G. process was successful is another issue that I will deal with later. The point here is that the main focus was getting hourly people involved. Many of you saw things being done to improve relationships between management and the union. Again, the focus was on hourly people. The unspoken message these activities transmitted to the organization was that employee involvement is for union officials and other hourly people. And that is why many of us believe this misconception. What needs to be understood is that employee involvement cannot reach an effective stage if it is confined to one or two levels of our organization and if it is not diffused evenly throughout all disciplines.

Let's move on to the next question. Why have some of us come to the conclusion that employee involvement means relinquishing power and allowing unqualified people to run the ship? Because in many cases that's exactly what we did, and that's the unspoken message that went to the organization. Many of us still think that participative management is a fancy term for permissiveness, but that's simply not true. We were new at this then, and a lot of mistakes were made. We must learn from those mistakes in order to strive for continuous improvement.

Why do some of us believe that employee involvement won't work? Because in our own individual perception, we saw a lot of things happen that we consider unsuccessful. But let's take a look at what one dictionary has to say about success. It defines success as the achievement of something desired. What was it we desired when we started the E.P.G. process? Was it fulfillment of our obligation created by the G.M./U.A.W. contract? Then it was successful. Was it saving a lot of money? Then some teams were successful and others were not. Was it the creation of a large number of teams? Then it was successful. Did we want to keep those teams functioning for a long time? Then it was not successful. Did any of those teams help you? If so, you probably think it was successful; if not, you probably think it wasn't. That's one example of why some of us believe that employee involvement won't work.

As I said before, we were new at this, we had good intentions, but whenever you try something new, it's normal to make mistakes. Let's not waste time pointing fingers and blaming each other, let's learn from those mistakes and continue moving forward.

Why do some of us believe this is a trend that will go away? Because we've seen other programs come and go. But let's take a closer look at this so-called program. If you look outside G.M. at progressive businesses at home and abroad, you see employee involvement and you see it working.

Why is it so difficult to make it work? It's difficult to change an established culture but that's what has to be done to implement employee involvement as an on-going, continuous process for improvement. Most of us have been taught to tell our people what to do and then to enforce it. If they don't respond the way we want them to, we provide negative consequences. We've learned to look at our subordinates as people who implement our decisions. I'm not saying that was right or wrong, but I will say it's not that simple. We must change the way we value people and their ideas. It requires management skill to make our own decisions and then manage the implementation. It requires leadership skill to draw out the best ideas from a workforce as large as ours, and then get those people to accept and implement those ideas with enthusiasm."

Employee Involvement is listed first among the "10" elements of synchronous manufacturing. If employee involvement is high, the other "9" elements can be accomplished with minimal disruption to the workforce. If involvement is not high, it will be a struggle for a small number of plant personnel (hourly rate, salaried, or an elected union official) to make the change process a "go proposition." Employee involvement is the easiest element to write about, but the hardest to attain.

Employee involvement can also pertain to plant personnel utilizing resources (man/machine/material) outside of the plant to solve in-house problems. At times, manufacturing problems are present that cannot be resolved with plant resources. An approach that we've used in solving these types of problems is local college resources. There are many university R&D programs active in G.M. today. At one time, there seemed to be a "stigma" that the academic world could not function outside of the classroom.

We had the good fortune to utilize University of Dayton personnel and facilities to resolve a process problem. Our success came about because of the fact that local resources were available when we needed them. These types of R&D programs promote trust and understanding between industry and the academic world.

Employee Training

The employee is represented by every person in our division. A continuous education process ensures that all our people have the skills and knowledge to implement synchronous manufacturing. A trained work force is a valuable asset. This concept has to be inherent in our thinking. The organization for training today is application-driven for understanding specific needs which include: problem solving, set-ups, process control, preventive maintenance, etc. "People are our future." We look at training as an investment.

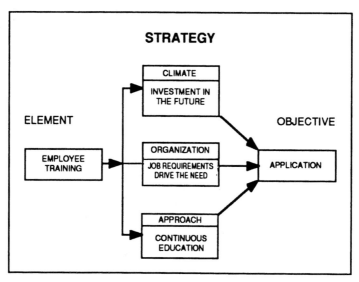

Figure 4

Based on what you're doing on your job, what do you need to do it well? The supervisor has to lead and be able to define tasks to be accomplished and define what training needs have to be met. Our plant took the position to train personnel to meet a need. We have utilized our joint training funds to the extent that we have applied to the *Reservoir Fund* for additional dollars required to meet our training requirements. Remember, *all* plant personnel need to first have an awareness of how their plant is run, before significant contributions can be made.

We are currently utilizing the "cascade" training process within our plant to "spread the word" concerning synchronous manufacturing concepts and measurements. The cascade training approach drives information from the "top" to the "bottom." Trainees receiving the information become trainers giving the information.

Man/Machine Effectiveness

Man/machine effectiveness requires an organization that moves toward improved material flow *(product focused* instead of our traditional *process focus)*. The required climate is one that allows for flexibility and the maximum utilization of people and equipment. Implementation requires flexible quality operators capable of running various pieces of equipment. It also includes equipment joined together to produce a family of parts that matches customer demand. The approach to implementation is elimination of non-value added elements of manufacturing. The objective of man/machine effectiveness is complete equipment/labor utilization.

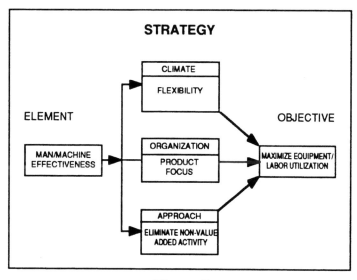

Figure 5

The traditional environment is process focused. A process focus is one that utilizes a group of similar machines such as a screw machine or punch press department to manufacture similar component parts. Normally, these machines are lined up, row after row, to produce their

parts. In the past, our manufacturing mind set was to group like equipment together, have one classification run the equipment (sometimes at a higher rate of pay), and then distribute the parts produced to the using departments via plant truckers. The results from a process focus approach were:
- Excess material handling
- Specialized workers
- Long lead times

Conversely, a *product focused* area will have whatever equipment is required to produce a sub-assembly or assembly for a customer. The equipment utilization is not as high as in a *process focused* area. Other benefits include less material handling and increased manufacturing flexibility.

Technology Guidelines

The following areas need to be addressed with regard to selection of process technology:
- Quality
- Unit cost
- Inventory
- Lead time
- Schedule compliance

Within these areas, there are certain processes that impact effectiveness:
- Operator control versus machine control
- Flexible change over capability
- Minimum amount of floorspace
- Simple work area
- Simple orderly flow of parts
- Complete product cycle (raw in, finished out)
- Multi-functional worker (quality operator)
- Employee involvement
- Efficient balance of equipment/labor

Depending on your customer requirements and process technology chosen, the outcome of these guidelines may differ. Example: comparing traditional automation with cellular technology (U-Cells).

Characteristic	Traditional	U-Cells
Machine Layout	Linear, Oval or L	U or Parallel
Production Rate	Fixed	Variable
Labor Assignments	Fixed	Variable
Cycle Time	Machine Control	Operator Control
Equipment Utilization	High	Medium-Low
Operator Utilization	Low	High
Material Movement	Conveyor/Pallet	By Hand
Production Run	Long	Short
Defects	Reop/Repair	Zero (prevent)
Changeover	10 Minutes-4 hours	1-9 Minutes
Batch Size	Large	Minimum of 1

If problems exist in a manufacturing area utilizing traditional automated equipment, a U-Cell may help reduce/eliminate the following problem areas:

- Multiple pieces of process equipment located throughout the plant(s) to process a product.
- Excessive trucking within the plant(s) to process a product.
- Highly variable schedules.
- Excessive changeovers/low volume required to meet customers' needs.
- A daily model mix being demanded each day by the customer.
- Poor utilization of multiple operations.
- Poor utilization of janitors/truckers.
- Large indirect labor force/salaried engineers required to support automated equipment.
- Boredom on the line.
- Excessive "buffer" stocks within the plant required to process a product.
- Excessive scrap due to quality problems—could be a misapplication of automation.
- The need to free-up floor space.
- Extensive P.M. required from skilled trades.
- Extensive downtime.
- Low equipment utilization.
- Excessive cost/piece caused by labor/burden.
- High retooling costs.
- Long lead time required to retool for a new customer.
- Synchronous scheduling not being used.

It is important to note that traditional machining and assembly equipment have a definite place in the manufacturing process. These lines provide part transfer that direct labor must assume in a U-Cell. If product volume is high or under a long term contract, the justification for traditional machining and assembly lines may exist.

If you are estimating a new product line and additional/new equipment is required, a U-Cell may be applicable if:
- Initial volumes are low for the first six months—two years, then increase, add labor as required.
- A minimal amount of floor space is available.
- You require operator control not machine control.
- A family of similar parts exists within a product line.
- Multiple changeovers will occur on a daily basis.
- All work can be done within the cell. No sub-assembly/component parts should be sent out of the cell for processing.
- A training area is needed to provide employee with total process knowledge of a product.
- The product line being produced is not fully developed.
- A simple/flexible work area is desired.
- Direct accessibility to tools/equipment is desired.

Again, neither automated equipment nor U-Cells individually solve all manufacturing problems. Each process technology addresses certain areas.

On the following page is an example of the "storyboarding" process that was used to determine if we should replace an automated assembly line with a low technology, operator controlled, U-Cell.

All of these items were brought up and discussed by a work group comprised of assembly department personnel, an elected union official, and various salaried resource people. Closer inspection of these items indicates the power of a group of people that can reach a consensus about the "right" things to do. Do you think that if one or two individuals came up with these exact same ideas, presented them to the same group, and implemented these items, the results would have been the same? Probably not, because of the lack of ownership, buy-in, and commitment. It is a funny thing how employee involvement weaves its way around the plant floor.

The McNellis Company Creative Planning Specialists Jerry McNellis, Director	720	**TOPIC** #1 Line Production U-Cell	U-Cell Team 513 Dept.	The Creative Planning Center 519 Ninth Street New Brighton, PA 15066 412-847-2120
Date: 5-7-87				Page: 1 of 4

HEADER	HEADER	HEADER	HEADER	HEADER
Goal of Cell	Goal of Cell	Workers for U-Cell	No Standard	Job Description
Subber	**Subber**	**Subber**	**Subber**	**Subber**
Customer Satisfaction Cost & Quality	provide a pilot area for 513 to run low volume & make schedule	019 classification via para 63B transfer	work to customer's schedule "weekly"	job rotation procedures
reduction of unit cost Level I	accomodate incoming outgoing just-in-time priciples	quality oper -no-	131 minimum per person to meet unit cost	unscheduled breaks. group will monitor activity
improve dept. Q.W.L.	employee to become aware of cost of product and help with budget	-003- no.		second shift to start at 2:48 p.m.
provide input for new business	provide input on new estimates			first shift to start at 6:18 a.m.
increase market share	provide sales department with a product that they can sell			need a leader to emerge from within
provide input to product eng. for booster "buildability"				Restricted phone for support help
make a profit				maintain records quality, schedule attendance piece cost

"Storyboarding" - The McNellis Co. - Creative Planning Specialists

Quality Control

Quality involves the total organization in: quality designs, quality suppliers, quality reports, a quality process, and quality operators. Quality is conformance to customer specifications and must be our first priority. The approach is to analyze the processes, attitudes, rules, etc. to determine if they are capable of consistently meeting customer specifications. Prevention, root cause analysis, and irreversible corrective action, will lead us to the objective of zero defects.

Are you working on the *symptom(s)* or the *cause*?

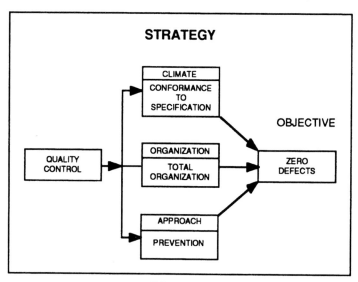

Figure 6

Many people have asked the question, "Why is the objective zero defects? Shouldn't it be customer satisfaction?" Our answer has been, if the objective is customer satisfaction, you may be sorting in your plant to meet this objective. You may even have to start at that point, but you want to move away from that type of a manufacturing attitude, to a zero defect attitude within your plant. This results in a customer satisfaction philosophy that you can afford on a day-to-day basis.

We've also found out that there is not *one* quality approach that corrects *all* problems. At one time control charts were the rage, then stop light gaging, and then design of experiments. Each approach has its own merits. Each works to solve certain problems. They are all good for the *right* application.

Set-up Reduction (Quick Change Tooling)

Set-up reduction requires that work groups analyze and improve the current process. Frequent changeovers are required for flexibility and batch sizes that match customer requirements. The approach is to establish a procedure that minimizes machine downtime. The objective is single digit or one-touch setups.

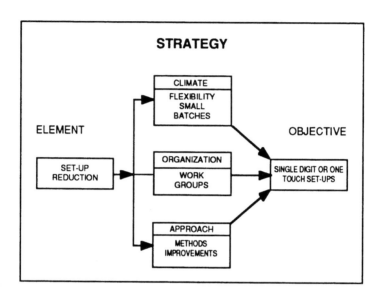

Figure 7

Since our plants need the ability to meet our customers' needs on a daily basis, the set-up reduction process helped us achieve that goal. To begin a set-up reduction process we had to understand our current set-up times. By definition, set-up time can be defined as:

"The time required to change from producing a part that conforms to the customer's specification at cycle time, to another part that conforms to the customer's specification at cycle time."

A simple definition could be *good* piece to *good* piece at *cycle* time.

NOTE: This definition holds true even if you are not changing to a different part number. If a die/tool becomes unusable, it must be replaced. The set-up time is approximately the same if you remove and replace a die/tool that produces the same part number.

Set-up reduction is important in a manufacturing facility because it will:
- Provide the flexibility to meet or exceed our customers' needs
- Reduce work-in-process inventory
- Reduce scheduling complexity
- Increase inventory turns
- Reduce scrap (reduced frequency of large scale defect problems in inventory, plus less trial processing)
- Makes changeovers easier for plant personnel

And requires:
- Increased Employee Involvement

The benefits of set-up reduction also include increased equipment utilization (greater percentage of gross cycle being obtained), cost avoidance of buying additional equipment, a reduction in the amount of capital equipment needed, fewer obsolete parts, freed up floor space, and reduced lot size. This enables your inventory to be "pulled" and maybe the greatest benefit is that it reduces a lot of the aggravation in making changeovers.

The first goal in our set-up reduction program was to reduce our current set-up time by at least 50%. Experience has shown us that an initial reduction in set-up time can be accomplished without a large investment. The second goal is another 50% reduction, which may cost more money, and the economic justification may be harder to attain. It should be noted that set-up reduction as a single stand alone project may be difficult to justify using traditional payback methods. Set-up reduction needs to be considered as part of an overall lead time (the time for the manufacturing process to occur) reduction process. The third goal should be to reduce your set-up time down to 10 minutes. This 10 minute changeover goal has been established because there is evidence that our competition is using this concept to meet their customers' requirements.

In some instances we can make improvements that will attain the *ultimate* goal of a "one touch" set-up, which is made in 1 minute or less. At the onset, this may seem to be a formidable task to accomplish. But, taking the opportunity to evaluate our current changeovers provided us with an insight on how it can be accomplished.

In my opinion, set-up reduction afforded our plant personnel the opportunity to react faster to changes in customer requirements. It was also the area in which we had to do the most work to play "catch up" with the rest of industry. We did not have new punch presses with rolling bolsters. Instead, we utilized simple basic technology that was available to modify our equipment to meet the goal of quick change tooling within *10* minutes, or one-touch set-ups within *60* seconds.

Preventive Maintenance

Preventive maintenance (P.M.) requires a commitment (availability of equipment) from all levels of manufacturing. Commitment is also required from manufacturing facilities to ensure that people and support equipment are available for scheduled downtime. Scheduled machine maintenance assures that our equipment is reliable and produces parts to

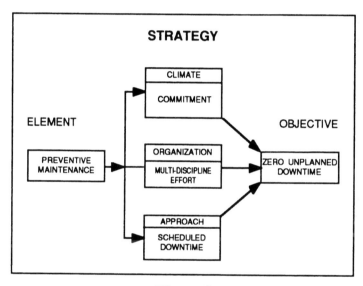

Figure 8

specifications when they are needed. The resulting increased machine uptime reduced the need for large safety stocks of inventory, resulted in increased productivity, and optimum utilization of all involved personnel. These efforts will result in minimal or zero unplanned downtime.

Think about the area in which you work or support. Can you list examples of P.M. in your area, department or plant? P.M. utilizes quality operators as well as skilled trades personnel. Both work together to form the support structure required to make this concept work. It is not just a maintenance problem, nor will maintenance alone provide all of the answers. Utilizing the quality operator concept enabled our plant to take advantage of all the knowledge on the plant floor. After all, who knows the equipment better than the personnel that operate that equipment.

Our entry into the P.M. program began with a computerized oiler's route throughout the plant. Since lubrication failures had been determined to be a major cause of machine breakdown and low equipment utilization. A good lubrication program is probably the most cost effective aspect of any P.M. program. Lubricants and the labor to service the equipment are among the least expensive items to support your P.M. program.

Since our plant does an extensive amount of aluminum and cast iron machining, we found that "off-shift" tool changes provided the two remaining machining shifts with a good base to work from. Machine operators like to know that their equipment is ready to run when they come in to work. A good start in the morning does wonders for an operator's attitude during the day. By the same token, a bad start at the beginning of the shift lingers throughout the entire shift. We also found out that a lot of the variables encountered with pre-set tooling can be avoided by having one person, or a small group responsibile for tool settings.

We've used both machine operators and skilled trades personnel to generate and modify our P.M. lists. Each item on a P.M. checklist has to be evaluated for validity and frequency. The continuous improvement program extends to the P.M. checklists. What *was* important to check daily may now be checked weekly and vice-versa.

There are probably many good "canned" P.M. programs and computer software on the market, but we took the position to develop our own program and related software to support our system.

If you are fortunate enough to have a computer-based system to work with, equipment histories should be generated in a data-base to provide historical data that you need to start your P.M. program. If you are experiencing poor equipment utilization on your machining lines (poor being defined as less than 75% of *gross cycle*), you have a tremendous opportunity for improvement. List your items by frequency and apply the Praeto analysis that all of us learned so well in our S.Q.C. training.

Ask yourself these questions: Have you or are you currently using vibration analysis and laser alignment techniques to increase equipment utilization? These techniques are not new in industry. It seems as though both of these areas got off to bad starts for one reason or another. We had a couple of false starts with vibration analysis ourselves. But, our maintenance personnel stayed with the equipment/technology until desired results were obtained. You may or may not be aware of the benefits of these types of maintenance aids. Take the time to make a few phone calls and save yourself the aggravation of re-inventing the wheel.

Preventive Maintenance can be justified as a cost improvement process. One of the first problems you will confront is the old adage "It don't pay!" Most people that make this statement do not have records that monitor equipment utilization closely enough. Manufacturing normally does not have documentation of equipment utilization (expressed as a percent of gross cycle), much less the catagories of downtime. This is not a criticism of manufacturing personnel, it's just that we have not provided them a system to monitor their equipment. Utilization (uptime/downtime) records are critical to monitor the continuous improvement process.

Supplier Relations (Certified Part Numbers)

Supplier relations promote a partnership between the manufacturing floor and the vendor. The climate is one of long term commitment between the supplier and their customers. The approach is one of total quality at the source driving us to the objective of part certification.

Part certification provides your vendor the ability to deliver their goods to your plant machining/assembly area, without any receiving inspection. Part certification is an earned reputation that a vendor must work hard to obtain. Part certification is a result of a vendor and a customer working together to achieve the desired result of a relationship based on

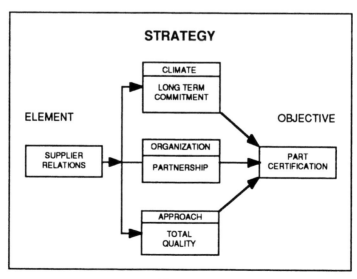

Figure 9

trust. The trust is earned by both the vendor and customer. The vendor must demonstrate to the customer, both machine and process capability, statistical quality control, and a delivery frequency that satisfies the customer over a period of time. Just because a vendor achieves that certification once, that does not mean he has a life-time certification. We currently audit a certified part on every tenth shipment.

Do you know of any certified part numbers that you have in your area? You have to stress that we need to become a certified supplier to our customer as well, and the customer might be the next department.

As stated previously, our manufacturing vendor and customer teams were an example of empowering plant personnel to accept the responsibility for their areas. Our vendors dealing directly with their customer (our manufacturing personnel on the machining and assembly lines), provide the climate, organization and approach for a win-win situation to exist.

After part numbers are certified, be sure to look at your part specifications. Are you demanding that vendors still meet old specifications that were required when you had one or two weeks inventory, versus one or two days?

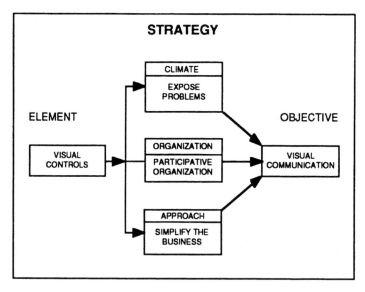

Figure 10

Visual Controls

Simply put, visual controls (management by sight) provide a "place for everything and everything in its place." Visual controls simplify the operation of each department. A joint effort is required to expose problems at all levels in the organization. A climate of exposing problems requires a participative organization dedicated to simplifying the business. The objective is clear communication, which supports problem identification and resolution.

Visual controls require a climate supportive in exposing problems. How much money does that cost? Probably not much considering the time and effort for a few signs in critical areas of the plant. You need to collect data and pick problems that involve a minimum of investment.

There are three basic types of visual control:
- Work place organization (low cost investment).
    Shelves/drawers for items needing storage
    Color coded containers
    Tools hung up so they can be found when needed

- Information
    Plant newspapers
    Job instructions (written by plant personnel)
    Process specifications
    Work group/team minutes

- Sensory/detection
    Equipment downtime clocks
    Proximity switches for container location
    (present/absent)
    Red/yellow/green lights

Can you tell, by walking through the plant, which operations or equipment are running as they should be? If not, what types of expensive support systems do you have in place to tell you what's going on? In our plant we have used the KANBAN card to provide plant personnel the information to determine if everything is in its place. KANBAN cards are both a visual and an inventory control item.

I once ran across a formula that I thought would be beneficial to use with a work group that could determine the correct number of KANBAN cards/containers to be used in a "pull" inventory system. The formula is shown below:

$$Y = D(Tw + Tp)(1 + f)/a$$

Y	=	Number of KANBAN cards/containers
D	=	Demand per unit time
Tw	=	Waiting time of KANBAN system
Tp	=	Processing time
a	=	Container capacity
f	=	Policy variable (fudge factor)

"D" is defined as a smooth demand. Average out the peaks and valleys in your customer's schedule.

"Y" is normally fixed, so if "D" increases/decreases, (Tw + Tp) must increase/decrease accordingly.

> Note: The "f" is determined by external factors such as lead times. Equipment utilization, % scrap etc.

I introduced this formula at one of the workgroup meetings. After I wrote the formula down on a chart pad, there followed approximately 30 seconds of uncontrolled laughter from the audience. Continuous improvement means learning from your mistakes. An important lesson here, do not use information that can't be used/interpreted by the customer.

Another lesson we learned is never try to implement a KANBAN pull system in a manufacturing process where you do not possess a high level of quality and process capability. If KANBAN cards are introduced into a system which lacks quality, all your cards may end up on scrap/re-op containers. You can't use too much care and planning when implementing these types of systems.

Synchronous Scheduling

Synchronous scheduling moves us away from "just in case" (push system) management to "just in time" (pull system) management. Stable schedules and a uniform plant load are a must to provide a pull system from one operation to the next. This method of scheduling provides an orderly flow of parts to meet customer demands.

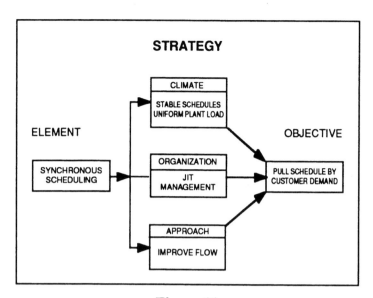

Figure 11

A traditional system is referred to as a "push" system. Run the computer generated schedule regardless of whether anyone needs it. The synchronous system is referred to as a "pull" system—a replenishment system—build only what the customer has used. Which one are you, push or pull? Do you have pull systems in place? Are they effective? Why? Historically, our plant personnel pushed inventory to their customer because our mindset was to generate direct labor dollars regardless of whether our customer needed the parts or not. Be ready for a dilemma on the plant floor when you start running to meet, but not exceed your customer's schedule. A question that you will have to resolve will be, what do you do with your people when your weekly schedule is complete on Thursday morning? You do not want to overrun the schedule, but people are available to work. Crew composition questions will start to arise. Traditionally we didn't let people just stand around!

The "just-in-time" synchronous scheduling concept is sometimes viewed as an inventory reduction tool. It's true that inventories can be reduced by this system. Long range, the benefit from this system comes from the establishment of an attitude to meet the customer's needs on a daily basis. Matching vendor capabilities with customer requirements will force your organization to improve quality levels, increase inventory turns, and reduce set-up times.

There have been many good books written about "constraints" (bottlenecks) on the manufacturing floor. There are even software packages available to create/solve many types of inventory scenarios. A thorough understanding of the constraints or limitations on your plant floor will have a significant effect on your individual scheduling approach. You can run into extremes at both ends of the spectrum. One extreme would be the plant with an excess supply of man/machine/material. If you have insufficient schedules to support your resources, what are your options—reduction of manpower, short work week, training, or transfers? Conversely, if you're short on man/machine/material to support your schedules, what is the result? Is it overtime, purchase of new equipment, or temporary transfer of manpower for a short period of time? How many times have you heard the comment, "We're either running too many or too few, why can't we have a balanced schedule?" Flexibility is the answer, but not an easy one to implement.

Even your tool rooms and maintenance areas have support and project workloads to address to meet their customer's (manufacturing) needs. Synchronous scheduling is *not* just a manufacturing and material control problem. We all share the same problems and can benefit from the same solutions.

Simultaneous Engineering

Simultaneous engineering is the gathering of a multi-disciplined group to design products that meet or exceed world class standards, resulting in meeting or exceeding our customer's needs. The climate and approach is established from design to production which ensures customer satisfaction. (See Figure 12)

This is our newest element of synchronous manufacturing. Within the next twelve months, we will be testing this element on our plant floor.

How many times have you heard, "Gee, product engineering did a good job of designing to meet or exceed customer requirements, but we *can't make it!*" This sometimes means quality is low and scrap rates are high or that the unit cost is higher than estimated. Does this sound familiar to you?

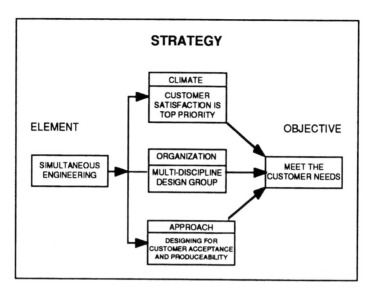

Figure 12

Our Vision

In 1986 our plant manager and his staff created a vision of continuous improvement that became our 5 year plan. At that time, plant personnel identified areas of improvement, that should be pursued. We originally started with 44 items to be completed over a 5 year period. In 1987 we had 94 items with 19 completions. In 1988 we had 236 items with 91 completions. In 1989 we currently have 315 items with 142 completions.

A vision (plan) is necessary to do business. You are guaranteed of one thing if you don't have a vision (plan). "Failure will come as a complete surprise."

The following is an overview of our 5 year plan. The format that we used was to address goals that we wanted to accomplish using eight of the ten elements of synchronous manufacturing. (See Chart on page 72.)

Overview of 5-Year Plan

ELEMENT	ACTION ITEMS	1986 JFMAMJJASOND	1987 JFMAMJJASOND	1988 JFMAMJJASOND	1989 JFMAMJJASOND
#1 Employee Involvement	Work groups implemented	xxxxxxxxxxxx	xxxxxxxxxxxx	xxxxxxxxxxxx	
	Absenteeism Controls Established	xxxxxxxxxxxx	xxxxxxxxxxxx	xxxxxxxxxxxx	
	Communication System Implemented		xxxxx		
#2 Man/Machine Effectiveness	Bottleneck Operations identified. On Floor. U-Cells Implemented	xxxxxxxxxxxx xxxxxxxxxxxx xxxxxx	xxxxxx	xxx	
#3 Quality Control	Capability Studies Completed Plant Quality Structure Implemented Plant Quality Teams Functioning Root Cause Teams Functioning.	xxxxxxxxxxxx xxxxxxxx xxx xxx	xxxxxxxxxxxx xxx xxxxxxxxxxxx xxxxxxxxxxxx	xxxxxxxxxxxx xxx xxx	xxxxxxxxxxxx
#4 Set-Up Reduction (Quick Changeover)	Current Changeover Times Determined Priority List For Improvement	xxxxxxxx xxxxxxxx	xxxxxxxxxx xxx		
#5 Preventive Maintenance	Data Collection Computerized PM Worklists Established Machining Process Assembly	xxxxx	xxxxxxxx xxxxxxxx xxxxxxxx	xxxxxxxxxxxx xxxxxxxxxxxx	xxxx
#6 Supplier Relations (Certified Numbers)	Part Certification (Productive)	xxxxxxxxxxxx	xxxxxxxxxxxx	xxxxxxxxxxxx	
#7 Visual Controls (Management-By-Sight)	Minimum of (1) Area For Each Department		xxx	xxx	
	Kanban System Implemented	xxxxxxxxxxxx	xxxxxxxxxxxx	xxxxxxxxxxxx	
#8 Synchronous Scheduling	Synchronous Scheduling Implemented MFG. Data Analysts Functioning STD. Containers Utilized (Pallet Pack)	xxxxxxxxxxxx xxxxxxxx	xxx xxxxx xxxxxxxxxxxx	x	

72 - Hard-Side Activities

This has been an overview of the synchronous manufacturing elements which support our continuous improvement plan. Hopefully, it has raised some questions that you need to answer in your plant, and provided an insight to some solutions that you might use in your plant. Remember, these synchronous manufacturing elements will only work if you have a solid support structure. This support structure allows empowered employees to do something over/above what they normally do on a daily basis. You have to continue to run your plant while making significant changes.

Chapter 9

OUR MEASUREMENT SYSTEM

Synchronous manufacturing requires continuous improvement to the process. The hallmarks of synchronous manufacturing include problem visibility, flexibility, process capability, product focused plants, pull production and reduced lead time. To achieve these ideals, we needed new measures of assessing manufacturing performance that were radically different from the traditional performance measures of just meeting shipping schedules and direct labor efficiency. Without adopting new measures of performance, the move to synchronous manufacturing would be hampered. Simply put, we needed a new scorecard.

Traditional manufacturing strategies emphasize minimizing the number of set-ups through long runs. The result is typically longer lead times, frequently at the expense of proper machine maintenance. Because the focus is on direct labor utilization, workers tend to become specialized. The traditional system demands efficiency in production, resulting in the manufacturing of products which cannot be used immediately (large inventory banks).

Stock piling of inventory becomes necessary to maximize direct labor usage when machines fail. Process capability becomes less important because the primary focus is on production. Investment in excess equipment is encouraged to ensure that specialized workers remain productive when equipment failures occur.

The result is high direct labor utilization with the potential of correspondingly high costs of non-conformance, excess inventory, excessive lead times, and personnel engaged in non-value added activities to inspect, repair, move, and maintain inventory.

Achieving world class status and meeting the customer's expectations requires monitoring our daily efforts in five key areas.

The primary measurements used to track the results of our synchronous manufacturing efforts are:

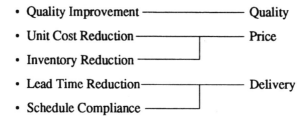

Synchronous manufacturing demands a completely new approach to *performance measurement*. Because it encompasses the total production system, measurement criteria must encompass the total production system as well. The measurement system represents your "scorecard" in the plant.

The ideal synchronous measurement system is based upon selecting representative performance levels which will drive an organization to be the best in the world.

It involves selecting key performance indicators, indentifying world class performance for those indicators, modifying strategic emphasis in manufacturing to meet selected performance goals, and continually measuring the organization's ongoing improvement trends. Success demands the commitment of the total manufacturing system.

Each level in the organization is responsible for the accomplishment of different goals; therefore, the measures of performance need to be different. To describe the various measurements and their linkage to each other, the following measurement triangle is used (see page 77).

First - at the top of the triangle, (level 1), is the objective of customer satisfaction.

Second - to stay in business the strategic product business units (SBU) need to pay attention to quality, price, and delivery.

Third - at the plant level, more detailed measurements of lead time, schedule compliance, quality, unit cost and inventory support the higher level measurements.

Fourth - inside the product at the superintendent level, more discriminating measurements may be added including total customer returns, operating expenses, process capability, and weekly schedule compliance.

Fifth - at the department level, measures such as lead time, set-up reduction, small batch sizes, area operating expense, planned vs. actual manpower, people training, flexibility, "presenteeism," etc. are added.

At each level, measures must be implemented that track the items needing improvement. Your "scorecard" needs to track improvements in

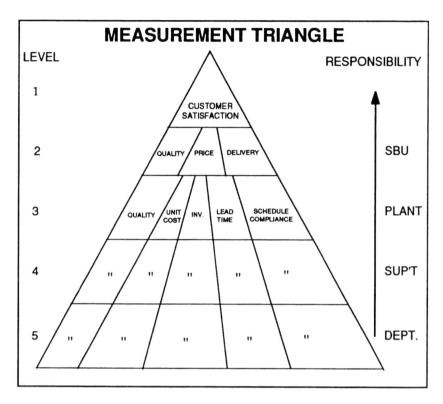

the areas of quality, unit cost, inventory, lead time and schedule compliance. To track improvement, you need to have a baseline or reference. In the past, we have not tracked unit cost, inventory, lead time, and schedule compliance nor reported to our bosses in these terms. Our old reporting system was based on how you were doing in your operating report and what did your direct labor look like in relation to budget. It is still important to manage and monitor your operating budget accounts and manpower, but the cost of our product lines is made up of more than labor, burden and processing supplies. Our mindset was to hold manufacturing personnel accountable for what they could control. Not a bad philosophy, but we found out that plant personnel can do so much more when empowered. Years ago, it was thought that only purchasing and product engineering could save money on raw materials. Today, we find that direct and indirect labor personnel can also help support the philosophy of certified part numbers and the decrease in the unit cost of raw materials or components that we purchase.

Hard-Side Activities - 77

QUALITY

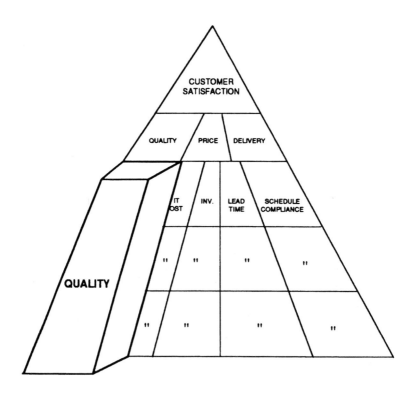

QUALITY

With regard to evaluating ourselves and how well we were doing in the area of producing a quality product, the world market forced our plant to review our quality rating system.

We were fortunate in that we had been working on machine and process capabilities for a number of years to improve the overall quality level within the plant. In the past, we thought that we were doing a good job producing parts to a 99 1/2% acceptance level. Suddenly, the world class community stated the quality level should be measured in P.P.M. or parts per million. The world class quality level was set at 500 P.P.M.. If you equate a 1/2% scrap level to P.P.M., it is equal to 5,000 P.P.M., or 10 times the acceptable level.

We determined that within our plant that the 500 P.P.M. could be obtained, in time, to our *external* customers. *Internally,* the 500 P.P.M. would be more difficult to obtain because of the number of dimensions that we check on each part number that we produce in each department. Our internal auditors perform "quality audits" on a daily basis within the departments. These audits are also used as a reference point to determine machine and process capabilities.

There tends to be a lot of mental anguish on the plant floor when you see quality auditor reports in the range of 5,000-15,000 P.P.M. for the week. You have to remember that internally the P.P.M. level may be 5 to 10 times that of your external customer. Do not be surprised nor discouraged with these high internal levels. All you are doing is providing yourself with a new reference level of quality. Remember too, the time to find a quality problem is within your plant, not your customer's dock or assembly area.

We currently report our *external q*uality level quarterly to the plant personnel. *Internal* audit figures are reported weekly and are displayed within the plant on our television monitors for all personnel to observe.

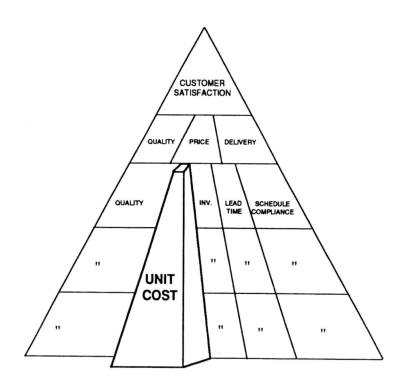

UNIT COST

Cost is an area that has historically been very confusing for most plant personnel to understand. At times, even the cost accounting personnel become overwhelmed by our corporate cost system. In the past, we have used such terms as:
- Variable Costs
- Fixed Costs
- Direct Costs
- Indirect Costs
- Full Factory Costs
- Commercial Costs

Since these terms are still being used by the accounting folks, we had a tough time on the floor determining the cost of a change. Our current accounting system has much "tradition" which some people (including some of our accounting people) consider excess baggage. For years costs were hidden within the walls of the financial community. It seemed that you had to have a security clearance to obtain facts and figures concerning the product lines that you were responsible for on a daily basis. Again utilizing the concept of employee involvement (yes, accounting personnel are real people too), we found that the present cost system was a bit too cumbersome to be used in departmental or work group meetings. Plant personnel, both hourly rate and salaried, can make many improvements to the product lines that they produce. These improvements can be made in all areas such as labor, labor related, raw material and commercial areas. What we needed was a scorecard to evaluate the cost trends within our plants.

Our accounting personnel responded by sensing our needs as a customer and worked diligently to come up with a simple cost model to gage the effectiveness of our change efforts. We all know this model as the "cost pie."

It became apparent to most plant personnel after seeing the cost pie that direct labor was not the largest piece of the pie, but the smallest. It was brought to the attention of management that if direct labor was the smallest portion of the pie, why did management always attack the labor portion for cost reduction? It was interesting to note that the answers included:

"Labor is the only item that we can control at the plant level."
"We can't change the raw materials."
"Labor is the easiest to change."
"Labor is the most visible."

With these comments in mind, our accounting department brought to the floor a new concept—Level III, Level II, and Level I costs.

By definition, Level III cost included cost incurred at the department level which included labor and labor related items.

Level II included the Level III costs plus allocated costs from support areas such as manufacturing engineering.

Level I included the Level II costs plus raw material and divisional allocated costs.

Though the Level I, II, and III cost structure is still not fully understood by all plant personnel, it was a big improvement over what we were originally dealing with. At least we could follow the Level II cost trends at the plant level regarding our product lines that we produce.

The Level II cost information is posted on plant information boards to promote the management-by-sight concept. Cost information is made available to all plant personnel and is updated on a monthly basis.

INVENTORY

To begin, from an accounting view, inventory is considered an asset; however, from a plant view, inventory should be viewed as a waste because it represents money spent and many times is just waiting to be used. Inventory can be misused. Many times it is used to cover up problems in a manufacturing process, and that's a waste of our scarce assets.

We measure the inventory in terms of dollars and inventory turnover. The value in displaying dollars lies in the awareness of the amount of money sitting idle. For General Motors, that is a staggering sum of money exceeding $10 billion in 1986. It should be easy to see that even though inventory is considered a financial asset, we are getting absolutely no return on that money, in fact, we must pay to have it in the form of taxes, interest, and insurance—what a waste.

Reducing inventory, resulting in a better turnover rate, can only be accomplished by eliminating problems and bottlenecks in the manufacturing process. Inventory dollars are reported monthly to plant personnel.

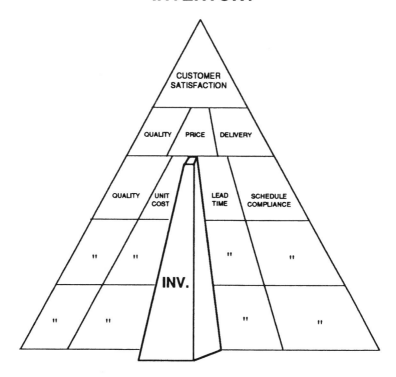

LEAD TIME

Previously, we discussed the three main measures of customer satisfaction: *quality, price* and *delivery*. Using the measurement triangle, the relationship of the 5 key synchronous measurements to customer satisfaction was displayed. In the diagram below, lead time is shown to have a direct influence on two of the elements of customer satisfaction—price and delivery. In the eyes of the customer, the shorter the lead time the better. Lead times are often longer than they need to be simply because it is more convenient if your organization does not have to be disrupted, and that can hinder our willingness to respond to requests made by our customers. In order to reduce lead time, our behavior must be driven by an attitude of wanting to maximize the benefits to both our organization and to the customer.

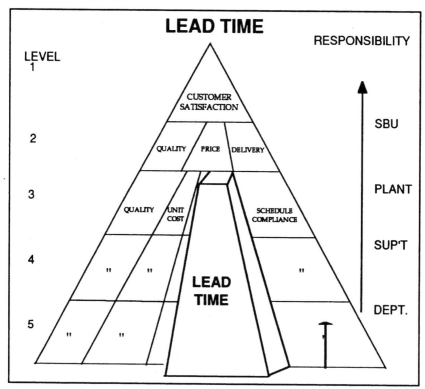

One way to get the customer what he wants is to carry enough inventory for him to choose from, but that requires an increased investment and increases the potential for obsolescence. Another way, a synchronous approach, is to stop doing the things we don't need to do.

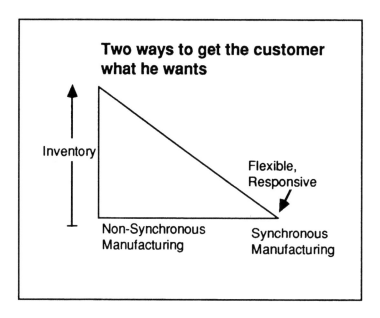

Traditional thinking taught us to believe that *more* inventory was *better*. What effect does inventory have on cost? How much inventory is enough? Did you ever ask, "With all this stock, how can we be out of the part we need?" Synchronous manufacturing requires improved flow—to be flexible and responsive.

As competition for buyers increases, so does the need to be flexible and responsive (fast and low priced). To maintain and increase market share in a consumer market means that auto producers and suppliers must be able to deliver what the customer wants, when they want it, and at the best price. Some of our practices are not very flexible or responsive and resulted from a time when the customer had no choice but to wait for the desired product. That environment led to an engineering, purchasing, and manufacturing approach that resulted in long production runs, minimum set-ups, high in-process inventories, etc.. Those times are in the past. Today our customers demand response-shorter lead times. To be world class requires each product or service to be produced the day it will be sold or used. That is the ideal—produce only what the customers want. Making more than can be sold or used adds to cost, is wasteful, and adds to lead time.

The difference between the ideal lead time and the actual lead time lies in the many problems in the processes that cause delays. Problems that cause long lead times cover the gamut—order-entry delays and errors, wrong prints and specifications, long set-up times, high reject rates,

Hard-Side Activities - 85

machine breakdowns, inaccurate schedules, inaccurate inventories, suppliers that are not dependable, long distances between operations, etc., etc. Everyone has a lead time for the product or service that they provide; only by solving problems can the lead time be reduced.

A measure of poor product or service flow is the amount of inventory in the process. By making improvements, and solving problems, inventory can be reduced. Lead time reduction is not solely an inventory reduction process, but rather a positive benefit and result. Previously, the 10 elements of synchronous manufacturing were reviewed and you saw that specific strategies and actions were necessary for each element in order to reach the objective. By assessing the lead time for the products or services that you supply, you will uncover the areas that need corrective action. Use the elements to guide your action list. Carefully think through each problem detected—what actions are necessary to create the correct organization, climate and approach. Note that lead time involves everyone in the organization.

Lead time within our plant is defined as the length of time it takes to get your product or service through your process. Lead time is expressed in minutes, hours, or days. Lead time is determined by adding together the process, move, store, and inspection time for each product or service.

The following items need to be understood:

No. Days Supply	Amount of available stock (inventory) at an operation divided by the usage rate. Example: Inventory of shoe and linings ahead of caliper assembly equals *10,000 pcs*. The daily usage rate equals *5,000 pcs*. The number of days supply equals 2. Another example could be the number of suggestions in your "in basket", divided by your processing rate, equals the number of days supply of suggestions.
Value Added	Value added operations are those that *change* part or document characteristics. Examples include: machining, painting, plating, press blanking, anodizing, welding, assembling, curing, heat treating, grinding, grit blasting, updating computer

	records, signing documents, creating P.O.s (purchase orders) and P.O. numbers, etc.
Non-Value Added	Non-value added operations are those that *do not change* part or document characteristics. Examples include: material/document movement, storing, and inspection.
Flow Chart	Pictorial displays of the material/document flow using symbols to represent operations, transport, store, inspect. In addition, color codes are used to highlight important points.
Process Time	Measures the time a part or document enters a value added operation until it is complete. Example: The time a part is loaded onto a piece of equipment until it comes off. Total process time is equal to the sum of each process operation time.
Lead Time	The process (value added) time plus the non-value added times.
% Value Added	A ratio of value added process time divided by lead time. The improvement efforts to eliminate non-value added activities, will move the ratio closer to 1—the ideal, or no non-value added activities.

Lead time is a simple method of identifying the problems in your area. Lead time can be reduced by solving problems. These problems range from poor quality, wrong specifications, long set-up times, insufficient inventory, excessive inventory, poor machine and process capability, long runs, poor coordination, poor communications, long transport distances, redundant reports, etc..

Lead time reduction is important in all areas such as Personnel, Marketing, Product Engineering, Accounting, Material Management, etc..

You should graph the lead time in your area, whether you provide a product or a service, as well as develop an action plan to reduce non-value added and value added activities. Continuous improvement and the elimination of waste is our survival.

SCHEDULE COMPLIANCE

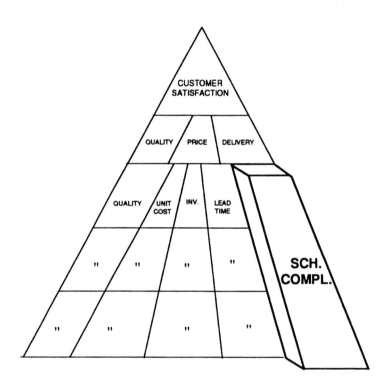

SCHEDULE COMPLIANCE

We need to understand the definition of scheduling and how we do it today, and concepts that will help us improve our performance. Scheduling, by definition, is the process used to achieve the customer's requirements by converting the demand into the components that make up the product and routing those components through the various fabricating, sub-assembly, and final assembly manufacturing operations within a specified time frame. The complexity of the car scheduling process is almost inconceivable; just think of all the materials required and all the manufacturing processes involved in making an automobile. Some who have studied this complex set of systems has described the process as a "daily miracle." To perform this miracle, requires that all parts be manufactured in the time frame designated on the manufacturing schedule. Non-conformance to the schedule can result in a dissatisfied customer and increased cost.

The schedule for all the component materials developed in the scheduling process is an authorization—it's ok to purchase material; it's ok to manufacture. Building without or in excess of the schedule has only one result...increased cost. The schedule is an image of what the customer wants and we can sell; if we cannot sell the product, it does not make sense to manufacuture it.

Making the schedule in the exact quantity and in the desired time frame that the customer wants can be difficult, and we, many times, make it more difficult by adding scheduling rules such as lot sizing, or by adding safety stock. Extra inventory or safety stock protects the manufacturing process "just in case" (J.I.C.) something breaks or the customer changes his mind. These added complexities can make the customers requirement look very different when you compare the schedule at the pack out operation to the starting fabrication operation, not to mention what your supplier's requirement looks like.

The concept of "uniform plant loading" is used to reduce "lumpy" schedules and reduce the costs associated with them. Uniform plant loading requires the development of an operations plan or master schedule that establishes the resource levels available—both manpower and machines. Inside the parameters established by the master plan the rule is to "make a little bit of everything everyday." The overall plant pattern and schedule is established by final assembly and all support departments must run at the same rate and sequence and thus, gets rid of lumpy demand.

Hard-Side Activities - 89

In the uniform loaded plant, since the pace of the plant is established by final assembly, that operation "pulls" needed parts from the supplying departments. Plants using the batch system "push" fabricated material to the using department. This is done even if the using department no longer needs or wants the material.

The opposite approach, as mentioned, is called the "pull" system and operates on the concept of consumption. Only replace or build what the user has consumed. When the customer withdraws material from the supplier that is the authority to manufacturer more. Can you see that with the pull system, we no longer need a computer generated schedule for each operation, expediting is eliminated, and inventory is reduced to a minimum?

Communication in the pull system requires a signal. This signal, which represents the authorization or schedule to build, can be passed on using a variety of different techniques: cards or labels (sometimes called "kanban cards"), special containers, electronic signals, lights, etc. The use of the pull system has been employed in several areas of our plant, but we need to be on a 100% pull system which includes our suppliers.

Our ability to be totally on the pull system requires an extensive look at our current process. If each operation cannot run at the same pace as final assembly, then we need to review the elements of synchronous manufacturing, and be making the improvements necessary in set-up reduction, preventive maintenance, quality and employee involvement.

We initially thought that our schedule compliance was in the "neighborhood" of 90-95% schedule performance on a monthly basis. But, when we took a good look at what we were doing internally in the plant, plus what we were shipping to the customer, we were surprised at how poor our performance was.

We found out that our schedule performance completion was really 3-5% of part numbers on schedule within the plant. We also found that we ran both insufficient quantities on some parts as well as excessive quantities on others. Graphically, we can show what we were doing in the plant. (See Graph A, page 93)

After reviewing the results shown on Graph A, we decided to provide ourselves a "scheduling window" to meet on a weekly basis. This schedule compliance window was equal to:

> 98%—102% of part numbers on schedule
> to our plants on a *weekly basis*.

In other words, if you ran less than 98% or more than 102% of what was on the weekly schedule, you missed the schedule.

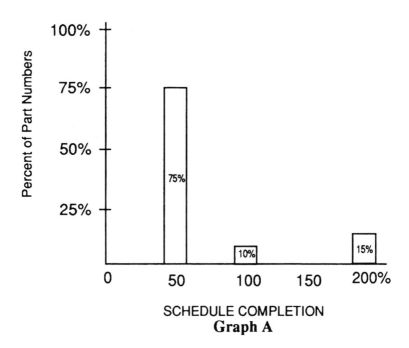

Graph A

Ideally, your graph should look like this.

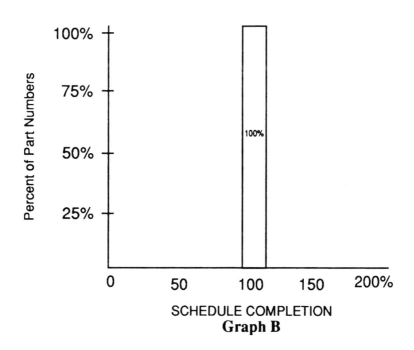

Graph B

Chapter 10

ACCOMPLISHMENTS TO DATE

No matter what kind of vision or game plan you have, you need to see positive results within your plant to know that you are doing the *right* things to become more competitive. We all know that we need to see postive results to provide additional motivation to do new and different things. (See Delco Moraine NDH's Road of Continuous Improvement chart on page 94.)

We feel that the ultimate victory was earning the right to manufacuture the General Motors ABS Brake System within our plant.

On pages 95-96 are a few of our Synchronous Manufacturing accomplishments to date.

DELCO MORAINE NDH'S
Road of Continuous Improvement

As you can see below, our vision consisted of a road to continuous improvement. As with any road, there are certain milestones that you pass which in our case initiated changes in our organization. As the roadmap indicates, we as a division started out from <u>two</u> different locations (philosophies), but came together to accomplish many positive plant changes which improved our competitive position.

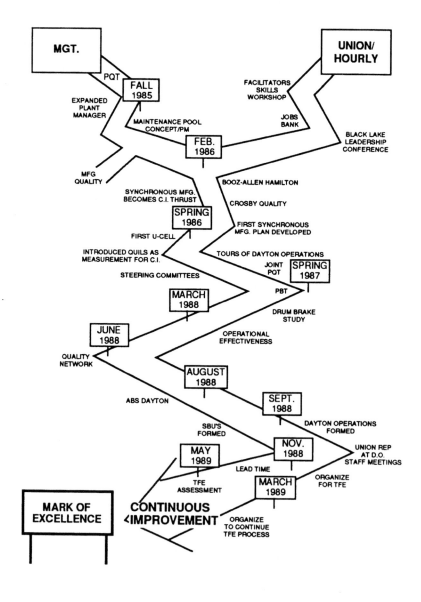

SYNCHRONOUS MANUFACTURING ACCOMPLISHMENTS

U-CELL-1

Item	Before	After	Gain/Reduction
Inv. Turns	12	100	317% Increase
Direct Labor			67% Reduction
Indirect Labor			25% Reduction
Distance Part Travels	45,000 ft.	2,500 ft.	94% Reduction
Schedule Compliance	75%	100%	33% Increase
Scrap Rate	10%	1/2%	95% Reduction
Floor Space	1480 sq. ft.	1024 sq. ft.	31% Reduction

U-CELL-2

Distance Part Travels	900 ft.	30 ft.	97% Reduction
Schedule Compliance	75%	100%	33% Increase
Floor Space	600 sq. ft.	100 sq. ft.	83% Reduction

Employee Involvement—Cell members designed layout and debugged cell.

U-CELL-3

Inventory Turns	12	20	40% Increase
Unit Cost (Front/Rear)			11% Reduction
Direct Labor			36% Reduction

Employee Involvement—Cell members designed, installed and debugged cell.

U-CELL-4

Distance Part Traveled	240 ft.	40 ft.	83% Reduction
Floor Space	12,500 ft.	2,500 ft.	80% Reduction
Schedule Compliance	80%	100%	25% Increase

Employee Involvement—Cell members designed, installed, and debugged cell.

Set-up Reduction (Quick Change Tooling)

1 1/2 hours down to 7 minutes	92% Reduction
5 hours down to 30 minutes	90% Reduction
4 hours down to 60 seconds	99% Reduction

During the past four model years 1985-88, a 38% cumulative performance improvement in our plant operating report.

Schedule Compliance - 1986/1987 — 3-5%
Schedule Compliance - 1988 model year — 45%

Inventory turns one year ago — 16
Inventory turns two years ago — 9-11
Inventory turns last month — 30

Salaried overtime reduced — 70%.
Hourly rate overtime reduced — 60%.

Equipment utilization increase
on dial index machine line — 67% increase.

Gearbox failure reduction by — 16%.

Plant inventory (raw + W.I.P. + finished) reduced by 40%.

 We have left many things unsaid for a lot of reasons but this adventure is not over. Our attempt was to present our "grass roots" level of experiences and not an "experts" handbook or cookbook. As messengers, risk takers and implementers we have enjoyed successes, agonized over "what ifs and taken direct hits." More importantly, we as a division have made progress toward our world class vision and have won some prizes such as the Saturn Power Brake Unit and Master Cylinder contract and the GM Antilock Brakes System Project (ABS). This reinforces our desire to be the "lead dog" in the brake systems business!

ABOUT THE AUTHORS

Charles Birkholz, author of Section I of this book, "Soft-Side Activities", is currently employed by Delco Moraine NDH as a Manufacturing Planning Administrator in the Antilock Brake Systems Group. Previous Delco Moraine work experience includes Manufacturing Operations, Production Control, Project Leader, Quality of Work Life Coordinator, Trainer and Human Resources Development.

He has designed and conducted facilitator skills workshops, team training and several offsite activities for Delco Moraine NDH employees both hourly and salary. Additionally he has helped conduct GM-UAW Leadership Conferences at the UAW Black Lake Training Center in Northern Michigan. He also has helped write and present papers at the 1985 IAQC Conference in Los Angles and the 1987 Conference in New Orleans centered around the participative process.

His education includes a B.S. and M.B.A. from Miami University, Oxford, Ohio along with GM organizational development workshops, university associates workshops and three IAQC Conferences. Workshop agendas included contracting, consulting, design, large systems change, leadership, impoving work groups and team building.

As he points out in Chapter Three, he was instrumental in designing and implementing communication, business, customer quality, and vendor quality teams with full hourly rate participation in his previous assignment. Coupled with this was the establishment of a plant joint steering committee which mainstreamed the ownership of our participative process.

Jim Villella, author of Section II, "Hard-Side Activities", is currently employed by Delco Moraine NDH as the Synchronous Manufacturing Coordinator for the Dayton Operations Plants. Previous Delco Moraine NDH work experiences include Manufacturing Operations as a first and second line supervisor, Production Engineer, and General Supervisor in Manufacturing Engineering.

His education includes a B.S. Degree from Miami University, Oxford, Ohio, along with numerous G.M. sponsored training programs.

Other Books on Employee Involvement

Productivity Press publishes and distributes materials on continuous improvement in productivity, quality, customer service, and the creative involvement of all employees. Many of our products are direct source materials from Japan that have been translated into English for the first time and are available exclusively from Productivity. Supplemental products and services include newsletters, conferences, seminars, in-house training and consulting, audio-visual training programs, and industrial study missions. Call 1-800-274-9911 for our free book catalog.

Championship Management
An Action Model for High Performance
by James A Belohlav

Many current books extol the values of being an excellent company. This book goes beyond that to explain how excellence can be achieved and why it is so critically important. A model for action demonstrates how any company can become a "championship" caliber company. Further, it explains why some excellent companies lose their edge while others remain excellent, and why still others appear to be excellent but are not.
ISBN 0-915299-76-3/272 pages/$29.95/Order code CHAMPS-BK

The Service Industry Idea Book
Employee Involvement in Retail and Office Improvement
Japan Human Relations Association (ed.)

This book presents an improvement proposal system in a context designed for customer service and administrative employees. Initial chapters about why suggestions are important and how to write persuasive improvement proposals are followed by two chapters of illustrated examples and case histories from various services industries and office or administrative situations. This is a creative book that should stimulate many ideas of your own. It is a companion to our best selling *The Idea Book: Improvement through TEI*.
ISBN 0-915299-65-8 / 272 pages / $49.95 / Order code SIDEA-BK

Better Makes Us Best
by John Psarouthakis

A short, engaging, but powerful and highly practical guide to performance improvement for any business or individual. Focusing on incremental progress toward clear goals is the key — you become "better" day by day. It's a realistic, personally fulfilling, action-oriented, and dynamic philosophy that has made Psarouthakis's own company a member of the Fortune 500 in just ten years. Buy a copy for everyone in your work force, and let it work for you.
ISBN 0-915299-56-9 / 112 pages / $16.95 / order code BMUB-BK

JIT Factory Revolution
A Pictorial Guide to Factory Design of the Future
by Hiroyuki Hirano/JIT Management Library

Here is the first-ever encyclopedic picture book of JIT. With 240 pages of photos, cartoons, and diagrams, this unprecedented behind-the-scenes look at actual production and assembly plants shows you exactly how JIT looks and functions. It shows you how to set up each area of a JIT plant and provides hundreds of useful ideas you can implement. If you've made the crucial decision to run production using JIT and want to show your employees what it's all about, this book is a must. The photographs, from Japanese production and assembly plants, provides vivid depictions of what work is like in a JIT environment. And the text, simple and easy to read, makes all the essentials crystal clear.
ISBN 0-915299-44-5/227 pages/$49.95/Order code JITFAC-BK

20 Keys to Workplace Improvement
by Iwao Kobayashi

This easy-to-read introduction to the "20 keys" system presents an integrated approach to assessing and improving your company's competitive level. The book focuses on systematic improvement through five levels of achievement in such primary areas as industrial housekeeping, small group activities, quick changeover techniques, equipment maintenance, and computerization. A scoring guide is included, along with information to help plan a strategy for your company's world class improvement effort.
ISBN 0-915299-61-5 / 264 pages / $34.95 / Order code 20KEYS-BK

40 Years, 20 Million Ideas
The Totyota Suggestion System
by Yuzo Yasuda

This fascinating book describes how Toyota generated tremendous employee involvement in their creative idea suggestion system. It reviews the program's origins, Toyota's internal promotion of the system, and examples of actual suggestions and how they were used. This account reveals the role of the Good Idea Club—an autonomous, in-house organization begun by gold-prize award winners, in fostering suggestion-writing ability. Personal accounts and anecdotes flavor the text, address problems encountered and their resolutions, and convey how trust and understanding became key elements of employee/ management relationships at Toyota. This case study will give any reader the inspiration to initiate a creative idea suggestion system of their own or significantly revitalize an existing one.
ISBN 0-915299-74-7/$34.95/Oredr code 4020-BK

CEDAC
A Tool for Continuous Systematic Improvement
by Ryuji Fukuda

CEDAC, or Cause and Effect Diagram with the Addition of Cards, is a modification of the "fishbone diagram," one of the standard QC tools. One of the most powerful, yet simple problem-solving methods to come out of Japan (Fukuda won a Deming Prize for developing it), CEDAC actually encompasses a whole cluster of tools for continuous systematic improvement. They include window analysis (for identifying problems), the CEDAC diagram (for analyzing problems and developing standards), and window development (for ensuring adherence to standards). Here is Fukuda's manual for the in-house support of improvement activities using CEDAC. It provides step by step directions for setting up and using CEDAC. With a text that's concise, clear, and to the point, nearly 50 illustrations and sample forms suitable for transparencies, and a removable CEDAC wall chart, the manual is an ideal training aid.
ISBN 0-915299-26-7 / 142 pages / $49.95 / Order code CEDAC-BK

Canon Production System
Creative Involvement of the Total Workforce
compiled by the Japan Management Association

A fantastic success story! Canon set a goal to increase productivity by three percent per month — and achieved it! The first book-length case study to show how to combine the most effective Japanese management princi-ples and quality improvement techniques into one overall strategy that im-proves every area of the company on a continual basis. Shows how the major QC tools are applied in a matrix management model.
ISBN 0-915299-06-2 / 251 pages / $36.95 / Order code CAN-BK

The Best of TEI
Current Perspectives on Total Employee Involvement
Karen Jones (ed.)

An outstanding compilation of the 29 best presentations from the first three International Total Employee Involvement (TEI) conferences sponsored by Productivity. You'll find sections on management strategy, case studies, training and retraining, kaizen (continuous improvement), and high quality teamwork. Here's the cutting edge in implemented EI strategies — doubly valu-able to you because it comprises both theory and practice. It's also amply illustrated with presentation charts. Whether you're a manager, a team member, or in HR development, you'll find The Best of TEI a rich and stimulating source of information. Comes in handy 3-ring binder.
ISBN 0-915299-63-1 / 502 pages / $175.00 / Order code TEI-BK

A Study of the Toyota Production System
From an Industrial Engineering Viewpoint (rev.)
by Shigeo Shingo

The "green book" that started it all — the first book in English on JIT, now completely revised and re-translated. Here is Dr. Shingo's classic industrial engineering rationale for the priority of process-based over operational improvements for manufacturing. He explains the basic mechanisms of the Toyota production system in a practical and simple way so that you can apply them in your own plant.
ISBN 0-915299-17-8 / 294 pages / Price $39.95 / Order code STREV-BK

Managerial Engineering
Techniques for Improving Quality and Productivity in the Workplace (rev.)
by Ryuji Fukuda

A proven path to managerial success, based on reliable methods developed by one of Japan's leading productivity experts and winner of the coveted Deming Prize for quality. Dr. W. Edwards Deming, world-famous consultant on quality, says that the book "provides an excellent and clear description of the devotion and methods of Japanese management to continual improvement of quality." (CEDAC training programs also available.)
ISBN 0-915299-09-7 / 208 pages / $39.95 / Order code ME-BK

Also from Productivity

TEI Newsletter TEI — Total Employee Involvement — can transform an unproductive, inefficient, even angry work force into a smart, productive, cooperative team. Learn how by reading the monthly TEI Newsletter. Its articles, interviews, suggestions, and case histories will help you promote a learning organization, activate continuous improvement, and encourage creativity in all your employees. To subscribe, or for more information, call 1-800-888-6485. Please state order code "BA" when ordering.

COMPLETE LIST OF TITLES FROM PRODUCTIVITY PRESS

Akao, Yoji (ed.). **Quality Function Deployment: Integrating Customer Requirements into Product Design**
ISBN 0-915299-41-0 / 1990 / 387 pages / $75.00 / order code QFD

Asaka, Tetsuichi and Kazuo Ozeki (eds.). **Handbook of Quality Tools: The Japanese Approach**
ISBN 0-915299-45-3 / 1990 / 336 pages / $59.95 / order code HQT

Belohlav, James A. **Championship Management: An Action Model for High Performance**
ISBN 0-915299-76-3 / 1990 / 265 pages / $29.95 / order code CHAMPS

Christopher, William F. **Productivity Measurement Handbook**
ISBN 0-915299-05-4 / 1985 / 680 pages / $137.95 / order code PMH

D'Egidio, Franco. **The Service Era: Leadership in a Global Environment**
ISBN 0-915299-68-2 / 1990 / 194 pages / $29.95 / order code SERA

Ford, Henry. **Today and Tomorrow**
ISBN 0-915299-36-4 / 1988 / 286 pages / $24.95 / order code FORD

Fukuda, Ryuji. **CEDAC: A Tool for Continuous Systematic Improvement**
ISBN 0-915299-26-7 / 1990 / 144 pages / $49.95 / order code CEDAC

Fukuda, Ryuji. **Managerial Engineering: Techniques for Improving Quality and Productivity in the Workplace** (rev.)
ISBN 0-915299-09-7 / 1986 / 208 pages / $39.95 / order code ME

Hatakeyama, Yoshio. **Manager Revolution! A Guide to Survival in Today's Changing Workplace**
ISBN 0-915299-10-0 / 1986 / 208 pages / $24.95 / order code MREV

Hirano, Hiroyuki. **JIT Factory Revolution: A Pictorial Guide to Factory Design of the Future**
ISBN 0-915299-44-5 / 1989 / 227 pages / $49.95 / order code JITFAC

Hirano, Hiroyuki. **JIT Implementation Manual: The Complete Guide to Just-In-Time Manufacturing**
ISBN 0-915299-66-6 / 1990 / 1000+ pages / $3500.00 / order code HIRJIT

Horovitz, Jacques. **Winning Ways: Achieving Zero-Defect Service**
ISBN 0-915299-78-X / 1990 / 165 pages / $24.95 / order code WWAYS

Japan Human Relations Association (ed.). **The Idea Book: Improvement Through TEI (Total Employee Involvement)**
ISBN 0-915299-22-4 / 1988 / 232 pages / $49.95 / order code IDEA

Japan Human Relations Association (ed.). **The Service Industry Idea Book: Employee Involvement in Retail and Office Improvement**
ISBN 0-915299-65-8 / 1990 / 272 pages / $49.95 / order code SIDEA

Japan Management Association (ed.). **Kanban and Just-In-Time at Toyota: Management Begins at the Workplace** (Revised Ed.), Translated by David J. Lu
ISBN 0-915299-48-8 / 1989 / 224 pages / $36.50 / order code KAN

Japan Management Association and Constance E. Dyer. **The Canon Production System: Creative Involvement of the Total Workforce**
ISBN 0-915299-06-2 / 1987 / 251 pages / $36.95 / order code CAN

Jones, Karen (ed.). **The Best of TEI: Current Perspectives on Total Employee Involvement**
ISBN 0-915299-63-1 / 1989 / 502 pages / $175.00 / order code TEI

Karatsu, Hajime. **Tough Words For American Industry**
ISBN 0-915299-25-9 / 1988 / 178 pages / $24.95 / order code TOUGH

Karatsu, Hajime. **TQC Wisdom of Japan: Managing for Total Quality Control**, Translated by David J. Lu
ISBN 0-915299-18-6 / 1988 / 136 pages / $34.95 / order code WISD

Kobayashi, Iwao. **20 Keys to Workplace Improvement**
ISBN 0-915299-61-5 / 1990 / 264 pages / $34.95 / order code 20KEYS

Lu, David J. **Inside Corporate Japan: The Art of Fumble-Free Management**
ISBN 0-915299-16-X / 1987 / 278 pages / $24.95 / order code ICJ

Merli, Giorgio. **Total Manufacturing Management: Production Organization for the 1990s**
ISBN 0-915299-58-5 / 1990 / 224 pages / $39.95 / order code TMM

Mizuno, Shigeru (ed.). **Management for Quality Improvement: The 7 New QC Tools**
ISBN 0-915299-29-1 / 1988 / 324 pages / $59.95 / order code 7QC

Monden, Yasuhiro and Michiharu Sakurai (eds.). **Japanese Management Accounting: A World Class Approach to Profit Management**
ISBN 0-915299-50-X / 1989 / 568 pages / $59.95 / order code JMACT

Nachi-Fujikoshi (ed.). **Training for TPM: A Manufacturing Success Story**
ISBN 0-915299-34-8 / 1990 / 272 pages / $59.95 / order code CTPM

Nakajima, Seiichi. **Introduction to TPM: Total Productive Maintenance**
ISBN 0-915299-23-2 / 1988 / 149 pages / $39.95 / order code ITPM

Nakajima, Seiichi. **TPM Development Program: Implementing Total Productive Maintenance**
ISBN 0-915299-37-2 / 1989 / 428 pages / $85.00 / order code DTPM

Nikkan Kogyo Shimbun, Ltd./Factory Magazine (ed.). **Poka-yoke: Improving Product Quality by Preventing Defects**
ISBN 0-915299-31-3 / 1989 / 288 pages / $59.95 / order code IPOKA

Ohno, Taiichi. **Toyota Production System: Beyond Large-Scale Production**
ISBN 0-915299-14-3 / 1988 / 162 pages / $39.95 / order code OTPS

Ohno, Taiichi. **Workplace Management**
ISBN 0-915299-19-4 / 1988 / 165 pages / $34.95 / order code WPM

Ohno, Taiichi and Setsuo Mito. **Just-In-Time for Today and Tomorrow**
ISBN 0-915299-20-8 / 1988 / 208 pages / $34.95 / order code OMJIT

Perigord, Michel. **Achieving Total Quality Management: A Program for Action**
ISBN 0-915299-60-7 / 1990 / 384 pages / $39.95 / order code ACHTQM

Psarouthakis, John. **Better Makes Us Best**
ISBN 0-915299-56-9 / 1989 / 112 pages / $16.95 / order code BMUB

Robson, Ross (ed.). **The Quality and Productivity Equation: American Corporate Strategies for the 1990s**
ISBN 0-915299-71-2 / 1990 / 558 pages / $29.95 / order code QPE

Shetty, Y.K and Vernon M. Buehler (eds.). **Competing Through Productivity and Quality**
ISBN 0-915299-43-7 / 1989 / 576 pages / $39.95 / order code COMP

Shingo, Shigeo. **Non-Stock Production: The Shingo System for Continuous Improvement**
ISBN 0-915299-30-5 / 1988 / 480 pages / $75.00 / order code NON

Shingo, Shigeo. **A Revolution In Manufacturing: The SMED System,** Translated by Andrew P. Dillon
ISBN 0-915299-03-8 / 1985 / 383 pages / $70.00 / order code SMED

Shingo, Shigeo. **The Sayings of Shigeo Shingo: Key Strategies for Plant Improvement,** Translated by Andrew P. Dillon
ISBN 0-915299-15-1 / 1987 / 208 pages / $39.95 / order code SAY

Shingo, Shigeo. **A Study of the Toyota Production System from an Industrial Engineering Viewpoint** (rev.)
ISBN 0-915299-17-8 / 1989 / 293 pages / $39.95 / order code STREV

Shingo, Shigeo. **Zero Quality Control: Source Inspection and the Poka-yoke System,** Translated by Andrew P. Dillon
ISBN 0-915299-07-0 / 1986 / 328 pages / $70.00 / order code ZQC

Shinohara, Isao (ed.). **New Production System: JIT Crossing Industry Boundaries**
ISBN 0-915299-21-6 / 1988 / 224 pages / $34.95 / order code NPS

Sugiyama, Tomo. **The Improvement Book: Creating the Problem-Free Workplace**
ISBN 0-915299-47-X / 1989 / 236 pages / $49.95 / order code IB

Suzue, Toshio and Akira Kohdate. **Variety Reduction Program (VRP): A Production Strategy for Product Diversification**
ISBN 0-915299-32-1 / 1990 / 164 pages / $59.95 / order code VRP

Tateisi, Kazuma. **The Eternal Venture Spirit: An Executive's Practical Philosophy**
ISBN 0-915299-55-0 / 1989 / 208 pages/ $19.95 / order code EVS

AUDIO-VISUAL PROGRAMS

Japan Management Association. **Total Productive Maintenance: Maximizing Productivity and Quality**
ISBN 0-915299-46-1 / 167 slides / 1989 / $749.00 / order code STPM
ISBN 0-915299-49-6 / 2 videos / 1989 / $749.00 / order code VTPM

Shingo, Shigeo. **The SMED System,** Translated by Andrew P. Dillon
ISBN 0-915299-11-9 / 181 slides / 1986 / $749.00 / order code S5
ISBN 0-915299-27-5 / 2 videos / 1987 / $749.00 / order code V5

Shingo, Shigeo. **The Poka-yoke System,** Translated by Andrew P. Dillon
ISBN 0-915299-13-5 / 235 slides / 1987 / $749.00 / order code S6
ISBN 0-915299-28-3 / 2 videos / 1987 / $749.00 / order code V6

TO ORDER: Write, phone, or fax Productivity Press, Dept. BK, P.O. Box 3007, Cambridge, MA 02140, phone 1-800-274-9911, fax 617-868-3524. Send check or charge to your credit card (American Express, Visa, MasterCard accepted).

U.S. ORDERS: Add $4 shipping for first book, $2 each additional for UPS surface delivery. CT residents add 8% and MA residents 5% sales tax.

INTERNATIONAL ORDERS: Write, phone, or fax for quote and indicate shipping method desired. Pre-payment in U.S. dollars must accompany your order (checks must be drawn on U.S. banks). When quote is returned with payment, your order will be shipped promptly by the method requested.

NOTE: Prices subject to change without notice.